FOUNDATIONS OF MODERN POLITICAL SCIENCE SERIES
Robert A. Dahl, Editor

MODERN POLITICAL ANALYSIS

Modern

Political

Analysis

FOUNDATIONS OF MODERN POLITICAL SCIENCE SERIES

ENGLEWOOD CLIFFS, NEW JERSEY   Prentice-Hall, Inc.

ROBERT A. DAHL

Yale University

Sixth printing. . . . . November, 1965

FOUNDATIONS OF MODERN POLITICAL SCIENCE SERIES

Robert A. Dahl, Editor

C59705

Preface

There are, as you may have discovered, enthusiasts
who appear to believe that most (if not all) important
knowledge about politics can be found between
the covers of a single book—or at least in the works of one author.
If you study my man X deeply enough, your enthusiast will
say, you will find that he tells you everything.
Your enthusiast's oracle is very likely
some great name: Plato, perhaps, or Aristotle,
or Machiavelli, or Marx. But for that matter, the oracle might
turn out to be some ex-sportswriter, now political pundit.
I am reasonably sure that this is false, and a
vain hope. It is a melancholy fact that no one has ever been
wise enough to contribute more than
a small fraction of what is known about politics.
That, at least, is what I believe.

Our enthusiast has a first cousin who insists that everything important has already been said in the great works of the past, as if wisdom must be aged, like wine, to make it better. Yet you may search as long and as hard as you like in the great works and you will not, I am quite sure, find as much about the operation of modern political parties, the American Congress, the political system of the USSR, or a great number of other topics, as you will find in recent studies.

For political institutions change. Modern democracy simply is not equivalent to the Athenian political system or the Roman Republic. Then, too, the study of politics is to some extent cumulative. Indeed on certain topics, knowledge increases almost annually. I have in mind particularly the study of political attitudes, of voting and elections, of political participation generally, where techniques of quite recent invention have revolutionized our ways of studying political behavior. If someone were to ask, "How can I learn about what sorts of people participate most in politics, and why?", I would urge him to start with the most recent studies in the field and work backwards. I seriously doubt whether he would get much help from Aristotle, Rousseau, or the *Federalist Papers*.

Yet, in my view, it is equally arrogant to suppose that very little worth knowing is to be found outside the more recent works. Recent studies often help us to gain a better judgment on questions of fact—and anyone who is contemptuous of fact had better forget about studying politics. Twenty-five centuries of dedicated study of politics have naturally produced a good many highly plausible but, unfortunately, contradictory hypotheses, each strongly supported by common sense, that can be argued till Doomsday so long as one sticks to the older methods of analysis. Happily, new methods of inquiry or analysis sometimes help us to settle these questions. Yet *all* the questions never do get settled; and probably they never will. This is one respect in which the best of the profound works of the past, even of the distant past, are invaluable. They make us aware of what these unsettled questions are. And they present us with the best fruits of creative minds struggling to arrive at answers. We do not know so much today that we can afford to neglect this older wisdom.

Now what, you ask, have these observations to do with a book on modern political analysis? This: Like the series of which it is a part, this book does not pretend to tell you all that you need to know about politics. Its aim is more modest but more realistic: to equip you with a small number of basic concepts, ideas, and analytical tools—ancient or recent, whichever seem the better—so that you can proceed afterward with more competence toward what should be, in a democracy, a life-long vocation: the analysis of politics.

Acknowledgments, were I to list them all, would require more space than is available. I would not, however, want to miss this opportunity to thank Alfred Goodyear, James Murray, and Wilbur Mangas of Prentice-Hall for constructive editorial advice and help.

Robert A. Dahl

New Haven
1963

Preface

Contents

ix

Contents

Some Unavoidable Political Questions

Whether he likes it or not, virtually no one
is completely beyond the reach of some kind of political
system. A citizen encounters politics
in the government of a country, town, school, church,
business firm, trade union, club, political party, civic association,
and a host of other organizations, from the United Nations
to the PTA. Politics is one of the unavoidable
facts of human existence. Everyone is involved in some fashion
at some time in some kind of political system.

Politics is necessarily an ancient and universal experience, and the art and science of political analysis have developed over several thousand years throughout many sections of the globe. In particular, political analysis has thrived in all cultures that have inherited the enormous legacy of that ancient people, few in number yet great in influence, the Greeks of the pre-Christian era. Like many other arts and sciences, political analysis achieved an extraordinary degree of sophistication among the Greeks some 25 centuries ago under the tutelage of Socrates, Plato, and Aristotle. Since their time every age in Western civilization has furnished a few great students of politics who have tried to answer certain fundamental questions.

In fact, it is no great exaggeration to say that all great political theorists whose works are of interest to us today have asked much the same questions about politics. Among the most important of these questions are:

1. What is politics? How do we distinguish politics from other aspects of human life? (Chapter 2.)

2. What do political systems have in common and in what ways do they differ from one another? (Chapters 3 and 4.)

3. What is the role of power and authority in political systems? (Chapter 5.)

4. How do men behave in politics? What are the distinguishing features of *homo politicus*—political man? (Chapter 6.)

5. What conditions make for stability, change, or revolution in different political systems? What is required if peace is to be maintained and violence avoided? What are the prerequisites for a stable democracy? (Chapter 7.)

6. What sort of political system is the best? How should we evaluate different political systems? (Chapter 8.)

The questions themselves are endowed with the child-like simplicity of all the most persistent questions of human life. The questions themselves are easy to pose, enormously difficult to answer. This book does not furnish you with the answers. Instead it provides you with analytical tools you will need in order to search for the answers in an intelligent way.

Is political analysis, then, a science? Or is it an art? I believe that it is both. To the extent that many aspects of political analysis are most easily acquired by practice and training under the supervision of a person already skilled in political analysis, it is an art. Whenever students of politics scrupulously test their generalizations and theories against the data of experience by means of meticulous observation, classification, and measurement, then political analysis is scientific in its approach. To the extent that this approach actually yields tested propositions of considerable generality, political analysis can be regarded as scientific in its results. As we shall see (Chapter 8), the extent to which political analysis should be considered an art or a science is a hotly debated issue among contemporary students of politics.

Skill in analyzing politics is not the same as skill in practicing politics. Sometimes the two do not go together. James Madison's speeches at the Constitutional Convention and his chapters in the *Federalist* demonstrate that he was as brilliant a political analyst as this country ever produced; yet he was a mediocre President. By contrast, Franklin Roosevelt had enormous skill, insight, and astuteness as a political leader and President; yet one could not find in Roosevelt's deeply moving messages, state papers, and letters an analysis of how he himself operated as President that seems as valid as the

Some Unavoidable Political Questions

analysis contained in several later studies by scholars.[1] Even if Roosevelt had tried to explain how he operated, could he have succeeded? The skilled artist is frequently unable to explain why or how he does what he does so superbly.

Sometimes, to be sure, skill in practicing politics does go hand-in-hand with skill in political analysis. Woodrow Wilson was an historian and political scientist before he was a politician. His *Congressional Government,* which he wrote in 1884 when he was 28 years old, is still widely read three-quarters of a century later. As governor of New Jersey and as President—at least during his first term (1913–1917)—Wilson also displayed a high order of skill as a political practitioner. Moreover, every skilled political practitioner must have some capacity for political analysis, even though he may be unable to explain what he knows. Then too, the rapidly increasing complexity of modern national and international politics requires a corresponding increase in the analytical competence of political leaders. The old-fashioned ward-heeler whose political knowledge was narrow and parochial is disappearing from American politics, in part because he cuts such a sorry figure against the backdrop of all the new, unfamiliar and highly complex problems in an age of nuclear energy and man-made satellites.

Perhaps the best reason for improving one's skill in political analysis, however, is that it helps one to understand the world he lives in, to make more intelligent choices among the alternatives he faces, and to influence the changes, great and small, that seem to be an inevitable aspect of all political systems. Consider, for example, some of the typical questions that confront an American citizen today.

About the local community in which he lives: Who runs my town or city? How democratic is it? Is it run by a "power elite"? How can I find out? How can I study and analyze the structure of power in my own community so that I can then be most effective?

About war and peace: Is "peaceful co-existence" with the Soviet Union possible? What conditions increase the possibilities for peace? For war?

About our friends and allies: Are the conditions ripe for a new European super-state? For an Atlantic community of nations?

About American policies toward the rest of the world: Can popular government be extended successfully to the newly emerging nations of the world? What would be required? For example, is rapid economic development necessary for popular governments to thrive in these countries?

These are important and difficult issues. In trying to arrive at a decision, a citizen has to make up his mind on matters over which there is bound to be controversy and uncertainty. How then can a citizen make intelligent decisions on issues of this kind? To repeat, the purpose of this book is not to decide questions like these but to present some analytical tools that will be useful when you try to make your own decisions.

[1] Particularly, Arthur Schlesinger, Jr., *The Coming of the New Deal* (Boston: Houghton Mifflin, 1959), Part VIII, "Evolution of the Presidency." Richard Neustadt, *Presidential Power* (New York: Wiley, 1960), Chapter 7, "Men in Office."

Some Unavoidable Political Questions

What
Is Politics?

Nature of the Political Aspect

What distinguishes the political aspect of human
society from other aspects? What are the characteristics
of a political system as distinct, say, from an economic system?
Although students of politics have never entirely agreed
on answers to these questions, they tend to agree on certain
key points. Probably no one would quarrel with

4   the definition of a political system

as a pattern of political relationships. But what is a political relationship?

On this question, as on many others, an important (though not always entirely clear) place to start is Aristotle's *Politics* (written circa 335–332 B.C.). In the first book of the *Politics,* Aristotle argues against those who say that "all kinds of authority are . . . identical" and seeks to distinguish the authority of the political leader in a political association (or polis) from other forms of authority, such as the master over the slave, the husband over the wife, and the parents over the children.

Aristotle takes for granted, however, that at least one aspect of a political association is the existence of *authority* or *rule.* Indeed, Aristotle defines the polis, or political association, as "the most sovereign and inclusive association," and a constitution (or polity) as "the organization of a polis, in respect of its offices generally, but especially in respect of that particular office which is sovereign in all issues."[1] One of Aristotle's criteria for classifying constitutions, as we shall see, is the portion of the citizen body in which final *authority* or *rule* is located.

Ever since Aristotle's time, the notion has been widely shared that a political relationship in some way involves authority, ruling, or power. For example, one of the most influential modern social scientists, the German scholar, Max Weber (1864–1920), postulated that an association should be called political "if and in so far as the enforcement of its order is carried out continually within a given territorial area by the application and threat of physical force on the part of the administrative staff."[2] Thus, although Weber emphasized the territorial aspect of a political association, like Aristotle he specified that a relationship of authority or rule was an essential characteristic of a political association.[3]

To take a final example, a leading contemporary political scientist, Harold Lasswell, defines "political science, as an empirical discipline, (as) the study of the shaping and sharing of power"[4] and "a political act (as) one performed in power perspectives."[5]

The areas of agreement and disagreement among Aristotle, Weber, and Lasswell on the nature of politics are illustrated by Fig. 1. Aristotle, Weber, and Lasswell, and almost all other political scientists, agree that political relationships are to be found somewhere within circle A, the set of relationships involving rule, authority, or power. Lasswell calls *everything* in A political, by definition. Aristotle and Weber, on the other hand, define the term "political" so as to require one or more additional characteristics, indicated by circles B and C. For example, to Weber the domain of the political would not be everything inside A nor everything in B (territoriality) but everything in the area of overlap, AB, involving both rule *and* territoriality. Although Aristotle is less clear than either Weber or Lasswell on the point, doubtless he would limit the domain of the political even further—e.g., to relationships in associations capable of self-sufficiency (C); hence to Aristotle "politics" would be found only in the area ABC.

[1] Ernest Barker (ed.), *The Politics of Aristotle* (Oxford: Oxford University Press, 1948), pp. 1, 110.

[2] Max Weber, *The Theory of Social and Economic Organization,* trans. by A. M. Henderson and Talcott Parsons (New York: Oxford University Press, 1947), p. 154.

[3] *Ibid.,* pp. 145–153.

[4] Harold D. Lasswell and Abraham Kaplan, *Power and Society* (New Haven: Yale University Press, 1950), p. xiv.

[5] *Ibid.,* p. 240.

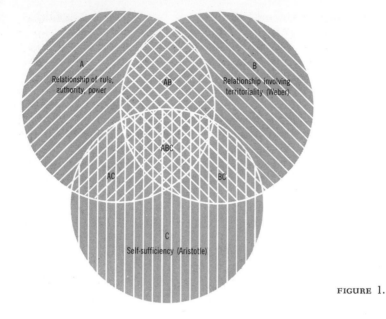

FIGURE 1.

Clearly, then, everything that Aristotle and Weber would call political, Lasswell would too. But Lasswell would consider as political some things that Weber and Aristotle would not: a business firm or a trade union, for example, might have "political" aspects. Contemporary students of politics do in fact study the political aspects of business firms, labor unions, and other "private" associations, like the American Medical Association.[6] Contemporary political analysis tends to accept, then, a broad definition of what is political rather than the narrower one of Aristotle. Let us therefore boldly define a political system as follows:

A political system is any persistent pattern of human relationships that involves, to a significant extent, power, rule, or authority.

The Ubiquity of Politics

Admittedly, this definition is very broad. Indeed, it means that many associations we do not ordinarily regard as "political" possess political systems: private clubs, business firms, labor unions, religious organizations, civic groups, primitive tribes, clans, perhaps even families. Three considerations may help clarify the unfamiliar notion that almost every human association has a political aspect.

1. In common parlance we speak of the "government" of a club, a firm, and so on. In fact, we may even describe such a government as dictatorial,

[6] Oliver Garceau, The Political Life of the American Medical Association (Cambridge, Mass.: Harvard University Press, 1941). S. M. Lipset, M. A. Trow, and J. S. Coleman, Union Democracy, the Internal Politics of the International Typographical Union (Glencoe, Ill.: The Free-Press, 1956). Robert A. Dahl, "Business and Politics," in R. A. Dahl, M. Haire, and P. F. Lazarsfeld, Social Science Research on Business: Product and Potential (New York: Columbia University Press, 1959).

6

democratic, representative, or authoritarian; and we often hear about "politics" and "politicking" going on in these associations.

2. A political system is only *one* aspect of an association. When we say that a person is a doctor, or a teacher, or a farmer, we do not assume that he is *only* a doctor, *only* a teacher, *only* a farmer. Probably no human association is exclusively political in all its aspects. People experience many other relationships than power and authority, experiences such as love, respect, purpose, dedication, shared beliefs, and so on.

3. Our definition says nothing at all about human *motives*. It certainly does not imply that in every political system people seek to rule over others, *want* authority, *struggle* for power, or the like. Indeed relationships of authority could exist even among people with no particular desire to exercise authority, or in situations where people with the most authority had the least desire for it. In American private clubs, for example, members who are the most avid for office are sometimes the least likely to be elected precisely because the majority of members prefer an officer whose desire for power is so moderate that he can be relied on to seek the views of others rather than impose his own on everyone else.

Some Critical Distinctions

Despite its breadth, our definition helps us to make some critical distinctions that are often blurred in ordinary discussions.

POLITICS AND ECONOMICS

Political analysis deals with power, rule, or authority. Economics concerns itself with scarce resources or the production and distribution of goods and services. Politics is one aspect of a great variety of human institutions; economics is another aspect. Hence an economist and a political scientist might both study the same concrete institution; but where the economist would concern himself with problems involving scarcity of resources, the political scientist would deal with problems involving relationships of power, rule, or authority. However, as with most attempts to distinguish subjects of intellectual inquiry, the distinction between politics and economics is not perfectly sharp.

POLITICAL SYSTEMS AND ECONOMIC SYSTEMS

Many people indiscriminately apply terms like "democracy," "dictatorship," "capitalism," and "socialism" to both political and economic systems. This tendency to confuse political with economic systems stems from the lack of a standardized set of definitions, from ignorance of the historical origins of these terms, and probably in some cases from a desire to exploit a highly favorable or unfavorable political term like democracy or dictatorship in order to influence attitudes about economic systems.

It follows from what we have already said, however, that the political aspects of an institution are not the same as its economic aspects. Historically, the terms "democracy" and "dictatorship" have usually referred to political systems, whereas "capitalism" and "socialism" have referred to economic institutions. From the way the terms have been used historically, these defini-

7

tions might be appropriate. (1) A democracy is a political system in which the opportunity to participate in decisions is widely shared among all adult citizens. (2) A dictatorship is a political system in which the opportunity to participate in decisions is restricted to a few. (3) Capitalism is an economic system in which most major economic activities are performed by privately owned and controlled firms. (4) Socialism is an economic system in which most major activities are performed by agencies owned and controlled by the government.

Each pair of terms rests on a dichotomy, and dichotomies are often rather unsatisfactory. In fact, many political systems are neither wholly democratic nor wholly dictatorial; and in many economic systems private and governmental operations are mixed together in all sorts of complex ways. While we shall leave the development of a more useful classification of economic system to others, in Chapter 3 we shall consider several ways of classifying political systems. Meanwhile, remember that the distinction between an economic system and a political system is indispensable to clear thinking.

DEFINITIONS AND EMPIRICAL PROPOSITIONS

No matter what terms we use, the two aspects of social life—the political and the economic—are different. However, like the central nervous system and the circulatory system in an animal, these two aspects are also interrelated. But the way in which the two aspects are related cannot be determined by definition alone: Empirical inquiry is necessary.

The failure to distinguish between a definition and an empirical proposition is common in political analysis. Yet nothing can be shown to be true or false about the real world of politics (or economics) simply by definition. A definition is, so to speak, a proposed treaty governing the use of terms. A sentence that employs such terms, however, contains an *empirical proposition* if it purports to say something about the world we experience. Whether the proposition is true or false depends on the degree to which the proposition and the real world correspond.

This point can be illustrated by considering the relation between economic and political systems. Assuming that we use these terms as they were defined a moment ago, four relationships would be logically possible.

	The political system is:	The economic system is:
I	A Democracy	Capitalism
II	A Democracy	Socialism
III	A Dictatorship	Capitalism
IV	A Dictatorship	Socialism

None of these combinations is a logical absurdity. None is excluded by definition. Whether each combination actually does exist, or is likely to exist, can only be determined by studying actual political and economic systems. Is it

What Is Politics?

true, as advocates of capitalism sometimes argue, that in industrial nations democracy could not exist without a capitalist economy? Is it true, as Lenin and other communists have argued, that a capitalist economy can exist only under a political dictatorship? Although questions like these are not always easy to answer, in principle we can do so only by examining all (or a fair sample) of past and present political and economic systems to see what combinations do or probably could exist. We *cannot* answer these questions by debating definitions.

Any collection of real objects that interact in some way with one another can be considered a system: a galaxy, a football team, a legislature, a political party. In thinking about political systems, it is helpful to keep in mind four points that apply to systems of any kind.

1. To call something a system is an abstract way (or as some scholars say, an analytic way) of looking at concrete things. One should therefore be careful not to confuse the concrete thing with the analytic "system." A "system" is merely an aspect of things abstracted from reality for purposes of analysis, like the circulatory system of a mammal or the personality system of a human being.

2. In order to determine what lies within a particular system and what lies outside it, we need to specify the *boundaries* of that system. Sometimes this task is fairly easy, as in the case of the solar system or the United States Supreme Court, but often it requires a somewhat arbitrary decision. For example, what would we consider to be the boundaries of our two major parties? Would we include only party officials? Or would we also include all those who register as Democrats or Republicans? Or those who identify themselves as one or the other, even though they do not register? Or those who vote regularly for the one party or the other? Later on, we shall see how the "boundaries" of a political system can be defined.

3. One system can be an element, a sub-system within another. The earth is a sub-system in our solar system, which is a sub-system in our galaxy, which is a sub-system in the Universe. The Foreign Relations Committee is a sub-system of the United States Senate, which is a sub-system within the Congress.

4. Something might be a sub-system in two or more different systems that overlap only in part. A college professor might be an active member of the American Association of University Professors, the American Legion, and the PTA.

It is useful to keep these observations in mind in considering the difference between a political system and a social system.

What is a "democratic society"? a "free society"? a "socialist society"? an "authoritarian society"? an "international society"? In what way is a social system distinguished from a political system?

These questions are difficult to answer because the terms "society" and "social system" are used loosely, even by social scientists. In general, however, the term "social" is intended to be inclusive; economic and political relations are specific kinds of social relations. Although the term "social system" is sometimes given a more specific meaning, it too is a broad concept. Thus Talcott Parsons, a leading American sociologist, defines a social system by three characteristics: (1) Two or more persons interact with one another. (2) In their actions people take account of how the others are likely to act. (3) Sometimes the people in the system act together in pursuit of common goals.[7] Obviously, then, a social system is very inclusive kind of association.

According to Parsons' usage, a political system or an economic system would be parts, aspects, or sub-systems of a "social" system. This way of looking at the matter is illustrated in Fig. 2., where AC represents the set of all political sub-systems, and ABC represents sub-systems that can be considered as either political or economic, depending on which aspect we are concerned with. Examples of ABC would be General Motors, the United States Bureau of the Budget, or the Federal Reserve Board.

Thus, the term "democratic" *society* properly describes a social system that not only has democratic political (sub) systems but also a number of other sub-systems that operate so as to contribute directly or indirectly to the strength of the democratic political processes. Conversely, an authoritarian society would contain many important sub-systems, such as the family, the churches, and the schools, all acting to strengthen authoritarian political processes. Let us consider two examples.

In his famous *Democracy in America* (1835) the illustrious French writer, Alexis de Tocqueville, listed a number of "principal causes which tend to maintain the democratic republic in the United States." His list included not only the constitutional structure but the absence of a large military establishment, equality in social and economic conditions, a prosperous agricultural economy, and the mores, customs, and religious beliefs of Americans.[8] In Tocqueville's view the prospects for a healthy democratic *political* system in the United States were enormously strengthened by the fact that a highly democratic Constitution was reinforced by many other aspects of the *society*. Hence American society could properly be called a democratic society.

By contrast, many observers were pessimistic about the prospects of democracy in Germany after World War II, because they believed that many aspects of German society were highly authoritarian and tended to undermine democratic political relations; they had chiefly in mind the wide tendency for social institutions of all kinds to take on a strong pattern of dominance and submission—the family, schools, churches, businesses, and all relations between government officials, whether policemen or civil servants, and ordinary citizens. The fact that political democracy had to be instituted in a predominantly authoritarian social environment was not particularly auspicious for the future of democracy in Germany. A number of recent observers, on the other hand, feel more optimistic about the future of political democracy in Germany precisely because they see evidence that the authoritarian character of other social institutions is declining.

[7] Talcott Parsons and Edward A. Shils (eds.), *Toward a General Theory of Action* (Cambridge, Mass.: Harvard University Press, 1951), p. 55.

[8] Alexis de Tocqueville, *Democracy in America*, 2 Vols. (New York: Vintage Books, 1955), Vol. 1, p. xx.

What Is Politics?

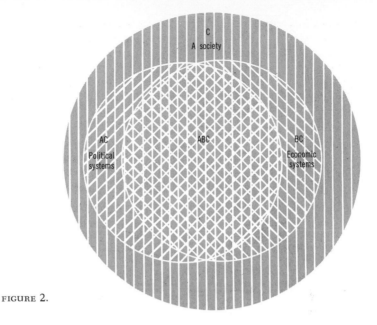

FIGURE 2.

Government and State

In every society, people tend to develop more or less standard expectations about how they and others will behave in various situations. One learns how to behave as a host or a guest, a parent or grandparent, a "good loser," a warrior, a bank clerk, a prosecutor, a judge, and so on. Patterns like these, where a number of people share roughly similar expectations about how to behave in particular situations, are sometimes called *roles*. We all play various roles, and frequently shift from one role to another very rapidly—e.g., the football player who attends classes before the big game, and then goes out with his girl afterward, has to shift almost as rapidly as a good broken-field runner among his various roles as student, competitive athlete, and suitor.

Whenever a political system is complex and stable, political roles develop. Perhaps the most obvious political roles are played by persons who create, interpret, and enforce rules that are binding on members of the political system. These roles are *"offices,"* and the collection of offices in a political system is what constitutes the government of that system. At any given moment, of course, these offices, or roles, are, aside from vacancies, filled by particular individuals, concrete persons—Senator Foghorn, Judge Cranky, Mayor Twimbly. But in many systems the roles remain much the same even when they are played by a succession of individuals. To be sure, in performing Hamlet or Othello actors usually interpret the role personally. So too with political roles. Jefferson, Jackson, Lincoln, Theodore Roosevelt, Wilson, and Franklin Roosevelt, for example, each enlarged the role of President beyond what they had inherited from their predecessors by building new expectations in people's minds about what a President should or legitimately could do in office. Nonetheless, at any given moment the role also defines and limits what the incumbent can do; Truman, Eisenhower and Kennedy were

11

all limited in various ways by their own beliefs and the attitudes of others regarding what role a President is supposed to play.[9]

But if most associations have governments, what about *the* Government? In the United States, as in most other countries, when you speak of *the* Government everyone seems to know what you mean. Of all the governments in all the various associations of a particular territory, generally one is in some way recognized as *the* Government. How does the Government differ from other governments? Consider three possible answers.

1. The Government pursues "higher" and "nobler" purposes than other governments. There are at least three difficulties with this proposal. First, because people disagree about what the "higher" or "nobler" purposes are that the Government pursues, and even whether their purposes are or are not being pursued at any given moment, this criterion might not be very helpful in trying to decide whether this or that government is *the* Government. Second, despite the fact that people often disagree over how to rank purposes or values and may even hold that *the* Government is pursuing evil ends, frequently they agree on what is and what is not *the* Government. An anarchist does not doubt that he is being oppressed by *the* Government. Third, what about bad Governments? For example, do democratic and totalitarian Governments *both* pursue noble purposes? That point seems logically impossible.

Our first proposed answer, then, confuses the problem of defining Government with the more difficult and more important task of deciding on the criteria for a "good" or "just" Government. Before anyone can decide what the *best* Government is, he must know first what the Government is.

2. Aristotle suggested another possibility: *the* Government is distinguished by the character of the association to which it pertains—namely, a political association that is self-sufficient, in the sense that it possesses all the qualities and resources necessary for a good life. This definition suffers from some of the same difficulties as the first. Moreover, if it were strictly applied we should have to conclude that no Governments exist! Aristotle's idealized interpretation of the city-state was very far from reality even in his day. Athens was not self-sufficient culturally, economically, or militarily. In fact she was quite unable to guarantee her own peace or independence; without allies, she could not even maintain the freedom of her own citizens. What was true of the Greek city-states is of course equally true today.

3. The Government is *any government that successfully upholds a claim to the exclusive regulation of the legitimate use of physical force in enforcing its rules within a given territorial area.*[10] The political system made up of the residents of that territorial area and the Government of the area is a "State."[11]

This definition immediately suggests three questions:

1. Can't individuals who aren't Government officials ever legitimately use force? What about parents spanking their children? The answer is, of course, that the Government of a State does not necessarily *monopolize* the use of force; but it has the exclusive authority to set the limits within which force may legitimately be used. The Governments of most States permit pri-

---

[9] For a comparison of differences in the way Roosevelt, Truman, and Eisenhower understood the Presidential role, see Neustadt, *op. cit.*

[10] Adapted from Weber, *op. cit.*, p. 154, by substituting "exclusive regulation" for "monopoly" and "rules" for "its order."

[11] Capitalized here to avoid confusion with constituent states in federal systems.

What Is Politics?

vate individuals to use force in some circumstances. For example, although many Governments forbid cruel or excessive punishment of children, most permit parents to spank their own offspring. Boxing is permitted in many countries.

2. What about criminals who go uncaught? After all, no country is free of assault, murder, rape, and other forms of violence, and criminals sometimes escape the law. The point is, however, that the claim of the Government of the State to regulate violence and force is successfully upheld, in the sense that few people would seriously contest the exclusive right of the State to punish criminals. Although criminal violence exists, it is not legitimate.

3. What about circumstances of truly widespread violence and force, such as civil war or revolution? In this case no single answer will suffice. (Remember the disadvantages of dichotomous definitions.) For brief periods, no State may exist at all, since no government is capable of upholding its claims to the exclusive regulation of the legitimate use of physical force. Several governments may contest for this privilege over the same territory. Or what was formerly a territory ruled by the Government of one State may now be divided and ruled by the Governments of two or more States, with gray Stateless areas where they meet.

We can be reasonably sure of one thing. When large numbers of people in a particular territory begin to doubt or deny the claim of the Government to regulate force, then the existing State is in peril of dissolution.

Conclusion

The question that heads this chapter has required us to focus on definitions and distinctions. But a person cannot acquire knowledge of the world by mastering definitions. We have defined politics so that we can distinguish it from other aspects of human life. We can now go on to explore the second great question posed in the first chapter: What do political systems have in common and in what ways do they differ from one another? In the next chapter we shall examine some ways in which all political systems, large and small, "public" and "private," democratic and dictatorial, tend to resemble one another in their behavior. Then in Chapter 4 we shall examine some of the important ways in which political systems differ from one another.

Political
Systems:
Similarities

In a number of respects, different political
systems display very similar behavior.
These empirical regularities occur not only in states
and governments but also in trade unions, business firms,
clubs, cities, and other political systems.
Of course, there are likely to be some exceptions
to any generalization about political systems. In this chapter,
however, we are going to ignore the exceptions in order
to concentrate on the run-of-the-mill.

Remember that the characteristics we are about to describe are not part of the definition of a political system. They are *regular characteristics* that you can expect to find in a large proportion of all political systems.

Characteristics of Political Systems

UNEVEN CONTROL OF POLITICAL RESOURCES

Control over political resources is distributed unevenly, even among adults. A political resource is a means by which one person can influence the behavior of other persons; political resources therefore include money, information, food, the threat of force, jobs, friendship, social standing, the right to make laws, votes, and a great variety of other things. There are four reasons why control over political resources is unevenly distributed in virtually all societies.

1. Some specialization of function exists in every society; in advanced societies specialization is extensive. Specialization of function (the division of labor) creates differences in access to different political resources. A secretary of state and a member of the Senate Foreign Relations Committee have much more access to information about American foreign policy than most citizens. An officers' cabal in the Turkish army has more opportunity to use the threat of force to gain its ends than a conspiracy among school teachers.

2. Because of inherited differences, people do not all start life with the same access to resources, and those with a head start often increase their lead. Individuals and societies are to some extent prisoners of the past; they never start with a completely clean slate either biologically or socially. Some endowments are biological. The fact that men are, on the average, physically larger and stronger than women means that men have access to more direct, primitive, physical force. And it may well be that the historic subordination of women to men is determined in large part by the fact that in a knock-down fight, men would ordinarily emerge victorious. Many endowments such as wealth, social standing, or the level of education and aspiration of one's parents, are not biological, however, but social. Whatever their source, differences in biological and social endowments at birth often multiply into even greater differences in resources among adults. Almost everywhere, for example, opportunities for education are related at least in part to the wealth, social standing, or political position of one's parents.

3. Variations in biological and social inheritance, together with variations in experiences, all produce differences in the incentives and goals of different people in a society. As a practical matter it is impossible for any society to provide everyone with a standard set of identical motives and aims, a kind of Do-It-Yourself Conformity Kit. Differences in motivation in turn lead to differences in skills and in resources: Not everyone is equally motivated to go into politics, to become a leader, or to acquire the resources that help the leader gain influence over others.

4. Finally, some differences in incentives and goals are usually regarded as socially beneficial because it is necessary to equip individuals for different specialties. If everyone wanted to be a full-time warrior, who would bear and rear the children? The circle is complete: Whenever specialization of function is regarded as advantageous, some differences in motives are also thought to be beneficial. But differences in motivations are likely to lead to

15

differences in resources—for example, to greater military prowess for warriors than for others.

For these four reasons (and probably for many others) it would be virtually impossible to create a society in which political resources were distributed equally among all adults. It does not follow, however, that there are no important differences in the way political resources are distributed in different societies. We shall discuss two critical kinds of differences in the next chapter.

THE QUEST FOR POLITICAL INFLUENCE

Some members of the political system seek to gain influence over the policies, rules, and decisions enforced by the government—i.e., political influence. People seek political influence not necessarily for its own sake, but because control over the government helps them to achieve one or more of their goals. Control over the government is such an obvious and familiar way of furthering one's goals or values that it is hard to imagine a political system in which no one sought power. The late American anthropologist, Ruth Benedict, in her well-known book, *Patterns of Culture,* suggested that the Zuñi Indians of the Southwest lacked virtually any striving for power. As a result, an elaborate ritual was devised for imposing the obligations of office on a reluctant member. But this situation is as rare as General Sherman's famous disclaimer, "If nominated, I shall not run and, if elected, I shall not serve."

It is important not to leap to the false conclusion that everyone who seeks political influence does so simply out of a desire for power as such. Although this conclusion is commonplace, the evidence against it is overwhelming. (We return to this question in Chapter 6.)

UNEVEN DISTRIBUTION OF POLITICAL INFLUENCE

Political influence is distributed unevenly among adult members of a political system. Clearly this proposition is closely related to the first one, which dealt with resources. For the fact that some people have more resources with which they *can* influence the government makes it easier for them to gain more influence over government if and when they *wish* to do so. Conversely, individuals with more influence over government can use their influence to gain control over more political resources.

The existence of unequal political influence has been a fact for centuries; yet though many observers agree on the fact, they disagree in appraising the fact, which is justified by some writers and attacked by others. The opening book of Aristotle's *Politics* sought to explain and justify the differences in the authority of master and slave, husband and wife, parent and child. Twenty centuries later in the midst of the Enlightenment, Rousseau (1712–1788) sought to explain and to attack inequalities of power in his famous essay, *A Discourse on the Origins of Inequality* (1755). Rousseau traced the origins of inequalities of power to inequalities in property. Inequality in property, he held, led in turn to inequalities in other resources. Less than a century after Rousseau, Marx and Engels put forth a similar explanation in the *Communist Manifesto* and a series of revolutionary works that followed. Interest in the origins of political inequality continues unabated to the present day.

Political Systems: Similarities

In 1938 Gunnar Landtman, a Finnish anthropologist, followed Rousseau's path by searching for explanations of inequality in an exhaustive examination of preliterate societies; his book bore a title that suggests both Rousseau and Marx: *The Origin of the Inequality of the Social Classes.* In 1951 an American political scientist, David Truman, observed that:

> Writers of the most diverse political views and using the most widely variant methods of observation have called attention to the existence in almost all groups of an active minority—identified by such condemnatory terms as "oligarchy" and "old guard" or such approving ones as "public-spirited citizens" and "civic leaders."[1]

The various reasons why political influence is always distributed unevenly in political systems seem to be reducible to three fundamental facts:

1. Because of inequalities in the *distribution of resources,* a point already discussed.

2. Because of variations in the *skill* with which different individuals use their political resources. Differences in political skill stem in turn from differences in endowments, opportunities, and incentives to learn and practice political skills.

3. Because of variations in the extent to which different individuals *use* their resources for political purposes. Of two equally wealthy people, for example, one may use more of his wealth to gain influence while another may use his to achieve success in business. These variations are themselves traceable to differences in motivations that evidently arise out of variations in endowments and experiences.

The causal chain might be illustrated as follows:

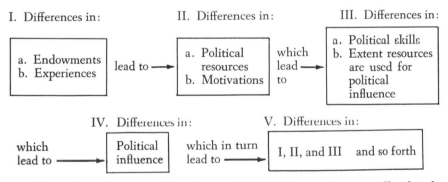

Sometimes the proposition that political influence is unequally distributed is confused with the hypothesis that in every political system there is a *ruling elite.* To say that political influence is unequally distributed does not imply, however, that a ruling elite exists. We shall come back to this distinction in the next chapter, for the presence or absence of a ruling elite is one respect in which political systems differ. However, if we call the individuals with the greatest political influence the *political leaders,* then our third proposition implies that every political system has political leaders. Although the term "leader" has a great variety of meanings in ordinary language, whenever we speak of leaders or political leaders in this book we mean the individuals with the greatest influence in a political system.

[1] David Truman, *The Governmental Process* (New York: Knopf, 1951), p. 139.

Some members of a political system pursue conflicting aims, which are dealt with, among other means, by the government of the political system. Conflict and consensus are both important aspects of any political system. People who live together never agree about everything, but if they are to continue to live together they cannot wholly disagree in their aims.

Although all political theorists have recognized this duality, some have placed more stress on the one than the other. Some, like Hobbes, have emphasized the propensity of men to conflict with one another; others, like Aristotle and Rousseau, their propensity for agreement and cooperation. Political theorists, like Hobbes, who emphasize the tendency of men to pursue conflicting aims are prone to stress the need for concentrated power and authority, obedience, loyalty, conformity, obligation, duty, and discipline. Theorists who emphasize men's immense talent for cooperation, like Aristotle or Rousseau, are more likely to stress how a political system, and particularly the State, can help human beings to pursue common goals, to win dignity and mutual respect, to share freedom, and to behave responsibly. Extreme views on the likelihood of cooperation and conflict are usually accompanied by extreme views about the State. Extreme fear of civic conflict is characteristic of totalitarian patterns of thought. At the other extreme, philosophical anarchists express unlimited confidence in man's cooperative nature.

The government does not necessarily intervene every time the aims and acts of different individuals conflict. Conflict is often dealt with by non-political means—by gossip, for example, or sorcery, or aggressive language, or even by isolated outbursts of violence. In many societies some form of personal combat is regarded as a normal way for men to deal with serious personal disagreements. Fist-fights, as everyone knows, were a common occurrence along the American frontier, and in some places they are commonplace even today.

In complex societies a good deal of conflict is mediated, arbitrated, suppressed, resolved, or handled in some fashion by political systems other than the State. But some conflict always remains to be dealt with by the Government of the State. Whenever a degree of coercion is required that goes beyond what is possible or permitted to other governments operating in the territorial area of the State, officials of the Government can use their superior power by virtue of the Government's exclusive control over the conditions under which violence may be legitimately employed. Thus the Government steps in whenever conflict is thought to be beyond adjustment by non-political means or by other governments than that of the State. In the United States, for example, the Government does not ordinarily intervene in labor disputes. But when prolonged conflicts between a union and management in a major industry such as steel threaten to weaken the economy, the President will probably intervene.

Some circumstances in which the Government of the State is likely to intervene in a conflict are:

1. When conflicts have serious consequences for third parties—as in the case of a strike in a key industry. In times of international crisis, as in war, the severity of third-party effects generally increases.

Political Systems: Similarities

2. When individuals act or threaten to act in conflict with norms so basic that organized and severe retaliation on behalf of the society is deemed necessary. In modern societies, murder, arson, theft and many other acts of violence are regarded as crimes punishable by the Government.

3. When conflict creates a danger of severe, prolonged, or widespread violence among members of the society.

4. When individuals in conflict do not share membership in any other political system capable of mediating the conflict, except the State.

THE ACQUISITION OF LEGITIMACY

Leaders in a political system try to insure that whenever governmental means are used to deal with conflict, the decisions arrived at are widely accepted not solely from fear of violence, punishment, or coercion but also from a belief that it is morally right and proper to do so. Belief that the structure, procedures, acts, decisions, policies, officials, or leaders of government possess the quality of "rightness," propriety, or moral goodness and should be accepted because of this quality—irrespective of the specific content of the particular act in question—is what we mean by "legitimacy." Thus, our fourth proposition is equivalent to saying:

Leaders in a political system try to endow their actions with legitimacy. When the influence of a leader is clothed with legitimacy, it is usually referred to as *authority*. Authority, then, is a special kind of influence, legitimate influence. Hence, our fourth proposition is also equivalent to:

Leaders in a political system try to convert their influence into authority. The phenomena of legitimacy are widespread and important. A writer as far-reaching in his curiosity as Max Weber saw fit to concern himself almost exclusively with legitimate governments and authority, evidently in the belief that power without legitimacy was too rare to be worth studying.

It is easy to see why leaders strive for legitimacy. Authority is a highly efficient form of influence. It is not only more reliable and durable than naked coercion but also enables a ruler to govern with a minimum of political resources. It would be impossible to rely on fear and terror, for example, to carry out the complex tasks of a large, modern, bureaucratic organization such as the Post Office, the army, Massachusetts General Hospital, General Motors, or the public school system of New York. It would probably also be impossible, or at any rate much more costly, to rely simply on direct rewards, for this would require an unwieldy "piece-rate" system. When a subordinate regards the orders and assignments he receives as morally binding, only a relatively small expenditure of resources, usually in the form of salaries and wages, is necessary to insure satisfactory performance.

Although many different kinds of political systems can acquire legitimacy, democracies are more in need of it than most other systems. For in the long run democracy cannot be forced on a group of people against its will; in fact, democracy is unlikely to survive even where a large minority opposes it, for democratic institutions would encounter rough going if a majority always had to impose its rule on a large minority.

An enormous variety of political systems seem to have gained considerable legitimacy in various times and places. Even in the relatively democratic society of the United States, political systems that reflect quite contradictory principles of authority nonetheless acquire legitimacy. For example, business

19

Political Systems: Similarities

firms, government agencies, and some religious associations are organized according to hierarchical rather than democratic principles. Yet citizens who concede legitimacy to the American government because of its democratic structure also concede legitimacy to these hierarchical systems. In times past, centralized monarchies, oligarchies, feudal institutions, and many other systems all seem to have gained some measure of legitimacy.

THE DEVELOPMENT OF AN IDEOLOGY

Leaders in a political system usually espouse a set of more or less persistent, integrated doctrines that purport to explain and justify their leadership in the system. A set of doctrines of this kind is an ideology. One reason why leaders develop an ideology is obvious: to endow their leadership with legitimacy—to convert their political influence into authority. And it is far more economical to rule by means of authority than by means of coercion.

Some leaders, including the highest governmental officials and their allies, usually espouse an ideology that justifies not only their own leadership but also the political system itself. Their ideology is then the official or reigning ideology. A reigning ideology indicates the moral, religious, factual and other assumptions that are assumed to justify the system. A highly developed reigning ideology usually contains standards for appraising the organization, policies, and leaders of the system, and also an idealized description of the way in which the system actually works, a version that narrows the gap between reality and the goal prescribed by the ideology.

In the United States, as every foreign observer since Tocqueville has observed for over a century and a quarter, the reigning ideology not only among leaders but among virtually all strata of the population is democratic.

A few years ago two political scientists conducted surveys of several hundred registered voters in Ann Arbor, Michigan, and Tallahassee, Florida, and found that almost everyone they interviewed held that democracy is the best form of government, every citizen should have equal opportunity to participate in government, the majority should rule, minorities should have the right to try to persuade others to their views, and so on. How deeply or knowingly these citizens believe in these principles is, of course, another question, but this survey and others demonstrate beyond question that with an astonishing unanimity Americans subscribe to the prevailing democratic ideology.[2]

Despite the fact that a reigning ideology helps incumbent leaders acquire legitimacy, it would be highly unrealistic to conclude that the existence or content of an ideology can be explained simply by the desires of leaders to clothe their actions with legitimacy and thus to transform naked power into authority. For one thing, the fact that many people who are not leaders accept the ideology reflects a desire for an explanation, an interpretation of experiences and goals, that offers meaning and purpose to human life and to one's place in the Universe. It would be surprising indeed if men who for thousands of years have sought to comprehend the relative motions of planets and stars in the skies did not also want to understand their own political order. Moreover, once a reigning ideology is widely accepted, the leaders may endanger their own legitimacy if they violate the norms contained in the ideol-

[2] James W. Prothro and Charles M. Grigg, "Fundamental Principles of Democracy: Bases of Agreement and Disagreement," *Journal of Politics*, Vol. 22 (1960), pp. 276–294.

ogy. They may even find it impossible to carry out their policies. For example, in 1936 President Roosevelt was re-elected by an enormous plurality. When the Supreme Court declared one key New Deal measure after another unconstitutional, he resolved to overcome the hostile majority on the Court by obtaining from Congress permission to appoint six new members. But he evidently did not anticipate the resentment such an attempt to "pack" the Court would generate, even among people who voted for him and supported his policies. In the fall of 1936 and winter of 1937, a sizeable majority of people evidently felt that the Supreme Court should be "more liberal in reviewing New Deal measures." Yet when the President unveiled his startling proposal in February, 1937, it was at once opposed by a substantial majority in Congress and a small majority among the general public. As the debate wore on, the magnitude of the opposition both in Congress and in the country increased. By June surveys indicated that 60 per cent of the people interviewed did not want Congress to pass the legislation.[3] In July the bill was killed. Roosevelt never regained the influence he had once enjoyed over Congress on domestic matters. Indeed, during the struggle over the Court, Roosevelt's northern Republican and southern Democratic critics in Congress learned how to form a coalition against the President, and this lesson they never forgot.

It would also be unrealistic, however, to assume that a reigning ideology is a unified, consistent body of beliefs accepted by everyone in a political system. In the first place, the extent to which a distinguishable ideology is actually developed and articulated varies enormously from one political system to another. Many political systems simply share the reigning ideology that lends legitimacy to the Government and the State. Thus it would be a good deal more difficult to specify the prevailing ideology among members of the United Automobile Workers or the Bell Telephone Company than among Americans generally. In the second place, probably no ideology is ever entirely integrated or internally consistent. For one thing, an ideology is not necessarily static; new situations create a need for new explanations and emphasis on new goals, and thus novel and unrelated or even inconsistent elements creep in. Then, too, a certain amount of ambiguity is sometimes a positive advantage precisely because it permits flexibility and change. The fact that Soviet ideology is ambiguous about how and when the final condition of full communism is to be reached permits Soviet leaders more free play than if a rigid timetable of specific steps were prescribed in the ideology.

Third, a reigning ideology is probably never uniformly accepted by all members of a system. Many members have only the most rudimentary knowledge of the prevailing ideology articulated by the leaders; others may actually hold—perhaps unwittingly—a variety of private views that are at odds with the reigning ideology. For all his insight and remarkably acute observations, Tocqueville undoubtedly exaggerated the uniformity with which Americans subscribed to democratic ideas in the 1830's. Certainly there is great variation among Americans today. The registered voters interviewed in Ann Arbor and Tallahassee were practically unanimous in adhering to the abstract principles of the American creed, but they disagreed sharply on a number of somewhat more specific issues—whether, for example, a communist should be

[3] For survey data, see Hadley Cantril (ed.), *Public Opinion, 1935–1946*, pp. 149–151, 755–757. For Roosevelt's proposal and strategy, see Joseph Alsop and Turner Catledge, *The 168 Days* (Garden City, N.Y.: Doubleday, 1938).

Political Systems: Similarities

allowed to speak or a Negro should be permitted to run for a local office. Moreover, for many people the reigning ideology, or indeed any ideology at all, is too remote, too unimportant, too abstract, or too complex for them to grasp except in highly rudimentary form.

Fourth, the reigning ideology may be rejected. Some members of a political system may adhere to rival and conflicting ideologies, as in the case of communists or fascists, in a democratic country, or democrats in a totalitarian or authoritarian country. Because people conflict in their aims, incumbent leaders rarely rule without incurring opposition, overt or covert; few systems can count on ungrudging support from all their members. Opponents of a regime often formulate criticisms that deny the existing system its legitimacy. Often, too, critics depict an alternative that, unlike the existing system, is held to repose on a legitimate foundation.

Sometimes the revolutionary ideology of one period becomes the reigning ideology of the next. In the eighteenth century democratic doctrine was revolutionary ideology; today, it is the reigning ideology in the United States and most of Western Europe. In Russia, Marxism and Leninism were revolutionary ideologies until 1917; since then they have become reigning ideologies, modified somewhat by Stalin and Khrushchev.

Because ideologies seem to rise and fall, and the reigning ideology of one system contradicts that of another, does one ideology possess just as much factual and moral validity as another? To anyone who finds the burden of choosing among conflicting views excessive, this view is seductive.

But for good or ill, political appraisal is not that easy. Properly interpreted, nothing that has been said so far—and, it is fair to warn you, nothing that will be said later—supports the notion that "all ideologies are equally valid." But this is a question we shall reserve for the last chapter.

THE IMPACT OF OTHER POLITICAL SYSTEMS

The way a political system behaves is influenced by the existence of other political systems. A political system rarely exists in isolation. One might think of occasional exceptions—a small and completely isolated club or tribe, for example—but these are so rare they can be ignored.

Exceptional cases to one side, every political system engages in *foreign relations,* for the actions open to one political system are affected by the past or probable actions of other political systems. A city cannot successfully ignore the existence of a national government; national governments must adapt their actions to the hard fact that other national governments, alliances, coalitions, and international organizations also exist. Even a club or a religious congregation cannot act with complete autonomy; and the leaders of a trade union must take into account the past or probable actions of business firms, other unions, and the government.

It is a curious fact that most people who portray their vision of an ideal political system ignore the limits imposed by the existence of other political systems. It is easier to imagine "the good society" if one does not bother with other, and quite possibly bad, societies that might clutter up the surrounding landscape. Consequently, political utopias are usually portrayed without the troublesome limitations imposed by foreign relations, which are eliminated by either ignoring them entirely or solving them according to some simple plan.

Political Systems: Similarities

In this respect the influence of Greek thought has been pernicious, for the emphasis of Greek political theorists on the virtues of a small autonomous self-sufficient State and their assumption that war was the natural and inevitable relation among States led them to ignore the usual problems of foreign affairs when States are not at war. In all Plato's *Dialogues,* which have had an enormous impact on Western political thought, there are only a handful of references to foreign affairs. Aristotle criticized Plato for the omission. "If a polis," he wrote in *The Politics,* "is to live in a political life [involving intercourse with other states] and not a life of isolation, it is a good thing that its legislator should also pay regard to neighboring countries."[4] Yet Aristotle had little more to say about foreign affairs than Plato. By contrast, in modern times the study of foreign relations has developed into a special branch of political science.

But how can we distinguish foreign relations from internal politics? How, in other words, can we distinguish one political system from another? What are the "boundaries" of a political system?

Fortunately, boundaries are usually assigned to a political system by *convention.* Conventional boundaries may be geographical. In this case everyone within the geographical boundaries is considered to be in that particular political system. Or membership may depend on some conventional characteristic such as paying dues, earning wages, being listed as a member or employee, or simply regarding oneself as a member, as in the case of many clubs and religious organizations. It is fairly easy to determine what the conventional boundaries are for the United States Senate, the Congress, the AFL–CIO, and the Benevolent and Protective Order of Elks.

Do boundaries of this kind rest on anything more than convention? Do they share a more general or abstract property? Is there any way of determining the boundaries of a political system other than by conventional usage? There is indeed, and in political analysis we often employ this criterion to determine whether the conventional boundaries coincide with the "real" boundaries of a political system. For example, Red China claims that its boundaries include Taiwan. In effect, Chinese leaders on Taiwan claim that their boundaries include the mainland. Now these moral, legal, or propagandistic claims would not necessarily be altered one iota by abstract political analysis. But it is possible to determine the boundaries of the political system that centers on Taiwan for purposes of analysis, regardless of whether these "analytical" boundaries are proper according to legal or moral criteria. You will recall that in Chapter 2 we defined a political system as any persistent pattern of human relationships that significantly involve power, rule, or authority. Hence, for purposes of political analysis, a boundary can be assigned to a political system *wherever there exists a sharp decline in the power of the government of the system to influence action.*

The reason why the 2500-mile border between Canada and the United States is not merely a conventional line on a map but a meaningful boundary between two political systems is—as everyone who crosses the border quickly learns—that the relative power of the officials of the American and Canadian governments over one's actions depends very strongly on exactly which side of the border one happens to be.

There may be many dips in the curve of power of a government; if so,

<hr>

[4] *The Politics, op. cit.,* p. 57. Words in brackets interpolated by the editor.

many different points might be regarded as the boundaries of a political system. Which set of points a person uses to bound a system depends on the particular question under analysis. For some purposes one might consider the political system of a trade union to include only those who regularly participate in meetings. But for other purposes one might include all those who accept the orders of leaders to go on strike, or all those who pay dues, or those who accept the authority of the leaders in any way at all.

One should not be overly disturbed if the boundaries of political systems are somewhat rubbery, for, in practice, conventional boundaries are usually sufficient. When they are not, a little attention to the problem one is trying to analyze, and some familiarity with the particular system, will usually indicate a number of satisfactory points which one can use to trace the boundaries of the system.

THE INFLUENCE OF CHANGE

All political systems undergo change. From time immemorial political observers have pointed out the mutability of political systems. "Seeing that everything which has a beginning has also an end," wrote Plato, "even a constitution such as yours will not last forever, but will in time be dissolved." With his characteristic preference for imaginative and somewhat rigid theoretical notions drawn from brilliant fancy rather than hard fact, Plato went on to describe the inevitable process of decay through which even the perfect aristocracy he proposed must degenerate into a "timocracy," or government of honor, to be followed in succession by oligarchy, thence by democracy, and finally by tyranny.

Aristotle rejected Plato's dialectic, but he devoted a lengthy section of *The Politics* to the causes of revolutions and constitutional change; he extended the theory of political change well beyond Plato, and, because of their solid good sense, his remarks are still worth reading today.

Yet although students of politics from time immemorial have observed the mutability of political systems, it is an interesting fact that those who set out to reveal the lineaments of an ideal State generally eliminate all change from their utopia. Being perfect, the ideal State either cannot change or, if it changes at all, must change for the worse. Consequently, political utopias exclude or deprecate the idea of change. Plato, as we saw, assumed that even his perfect State would change—but it must inevitably decay into increasingly degenerate forms. (As Aristotle somewhat testily pointed out, "When it comes to tyrannies, Plato stops: he never explains whether they do, or do not, change, nor, if they do, why they do so, or into what constitution they change.") Karl Marx turned Plato around. Marx portrayed the whole of history as ceaseless and ineluctable change. Yet once the final state of communism was reached, all the historical forces that had hitherto made for change were, presumably, to vanish. Even democrats sometimes imply that democracy is a final stage in man's political evolution.

Yet in the entire history of political institutions, no political system has ever been immutable.

24

Political
Systems:
Differences

The Multiplicity of Criteria

The differences among political systems
are more important to most of us than their similarities.
It is the real or presumed differences in political systems
that make one precious and another hateful. Human beings
have to live in political systems; but they do not have to
admire them equally. How, then, can we distinguish
one political system from another? Obviously there

are thousands of different possible criteria. Out of all these, which criteria we find most useful depends on the aspects of politics in which we are most interested. A geographer might distinguish political systems according to the area they occupy, a demographer by the number of persons who are members, a lawyer according to their legal codes. A philosopher or theologian interested in distinguishing "the best" political system will use ethical or religious criteria. A social scientist interested in determining how revolution is related to economic conditions might classify political systems by relative income and frequency of revolutions. Just as there is no one best way of classifying people, so no single way of distinguishing and classifying political systems is superior to others for all purposes.

Two Famous Schemes

ARISTOTLE'S CLASSIFICATION

Aristotle's classification has, however, proved so useful for so many different purposes that it has survived the political vicissitudes and transformations of 25 centuries. Indeed, it or something like it is as much a part of the habitual thinking of the student of politics today as it was to the observant Greek in Aristotle's day.

Aristotle proposed two criteria for distinguishing States or "constitutions." (These criteria can be applied not only to States but to political systems in general.) The criteria were "the nature of the end for which the State exists," and "the various kinds of authority to which men and their associations are subject."[1]

Aristotle used the first criterion to distinguish between systems in which the rulers govern in "the common interest," in which, that is, they seek the "good life" not simply for themselves but for everyone in the system; and systems in which the rulers pursue their own selfish interests rather than "the common interest." The first he regarded as "right" constitutions, the second, as "wrong" constitutions, or perversions of the first type. Aristotle used the second criterion to distinguish systems according to the relative number of citizens who were entitled to rule; in this way he arrived at the familiar distinction between the rule of One, Few, or Many.

On this basis we may say that when the One, or the Few, or the Many, rule with a view to the common interest, the constitutions under which they rule must necessarily be right constitutions. On the other hand the constitutions directed to the personal interest of the One, or the Few, or the Many, must necessarily be perversions.[2]

Thus Aristotle produced a famous six-fold classification illustrated in the table on the next page.

Two aspects of this scheme are particularly interesting. First, Aristotle combined both *empirical* and *normative* criteria in his classification; that is, his classification is not intended merely to describe what *is* but also to instruct us about what *ought* to be. To classify a political system according to

[1] Ernest Barker (ed.), *The Politics of Aristotle* (Oxford: Oxford University Press, 1948), Book III, Chapters VI and VIII, pp. 110 f.
[2] *Ibid.*, p. 114.

Political Systems: Differences

Rulers rule in the interests of:

		All	Themselves
The number of citizens entitled to rule is:	One	Kingship (Monarchy)	Tyranny
	Few	Aristocracy	Oligarchy
	Many	"Polity"	Democracy

the criterion of number is, in principle, a matter of observation. Whether one person, a few, or many rule in a specific political system is a question of fact (verifying what *exists*) and not a question of value (determining what *ought* to exist). On the other hand, to classify a system according to the second criterion involves a mixture of both fact and value. One must not only observe the actions of rulers in order to learn what the aims or consequences of their actions *are* but also appraise their actions according to some criterion of "interest" or "rightness" so that one could say whether or not these actions are what they ought to be. To judge whether rulers rule in their own interests or those of "all," then, requires standards of value.

In the second place, Aristotle gave the name "democracy" to the perverted form of popular rule, whereas in his day as in ours adherents of democracy would insist that what they mean by "democracy" is the rule of Many in the interests of all. Aristotle, however, held a slightly jaundiced view of Athenian democracy; like many later conservatives, he feared that the rule of the Many would typically lead to the tyranny of a poor and propertyless majority over the middle classes. As often happens in political discussions, Aristotle may have intended to discredit the term "democracy" by defining it as a perverse rather than a good form of government.

Curiously enough, Aristotle was dissatisfied with his own classification scheme. For he assumed it to be a fact that the Many would usually be poor and the rich would be few. Consequently (he went on to argue) the criterion of number was unsatisfactory; the essential characteristic was really the ownership of property:

The real ground of the difference between oligarchy and democracy is poverty and riches. It is inevitable that any constitution should be an oligarchy if the rulers under it are rulers in virtue of riches, whether they are few or many; and it is equally inevitable that a constitution under which the poor rule should be a democracy.[3]

In introducing differences in property or social class as a criterion for distinguishing political systems, Aristotle muddled his original classification scheme. Yet the price may have been worth it, for he was calling attention, though in a somewhat unclear manner, to a highly important hypothesis: namely, that the amount of power and influence members of a political system have depends on how much income, wealth, and social status they have. To the extent that income, wealth, and status are distributed differently in different systems, then we should expect differences in the way power is dis-

[3] *Ibid.*, p. 116.

tributed in each system. Thus Aristotle sought not only to *classify* political systems according to certain key differences but also to *explain* how these differences arose.

Where Aristotle was concerned with the numbers and social positions of rulers and the character of their authority, Max Weber devoted himself almost exclusively to the nature of the authority held by the rulers. In fact, as mentioned earlier, Weber restricted his attention to systems in which the government was accepted as legitimate.

Weber suggested that the leaders of a political system might claim legitimacy for their rule, and members might accept their claims, on three grounds:[4]

1. *Tradition.* In this case legitimacy rests "on an established belief in the sanctity of immemorial traditions" and in the need to obey leaders who exercise authority according to the traditions. Weber held that this was "the most universal and primitive case" of authority. But even modern systems acquire a good deal of legitimacy from their traditions. In few countries has political tradition had more influence than in England. Many aspects of modern British politics, such as the monarchy, are accepted by British subjects today because of immemorial tradition—after all "England has always had a monarch." Probably every stable political system gains some measure of legitimacy through the workings of tradition. Even in the United States, where people sometimes take pride in their freedom from tradition, political practices are often defended on purely traditional grounds. The right of the Supreme Court to declare acts of Congress unconstitutional cannot be found anywhere in the Constitution. Yet few Americans propose to take this right away, and doubtless many would defend the institution by saying that "this is the way it has always been."

2. *Exceptional Personal Qualities.* In this case legitimacy is based on "devotion to the specific and exceptional sanctity, heroism, or exemplary character of an individual person" and the moral or political order he has revealed or ordained. This is the kind of legitimacy the inspirational leader gains for his leadership—Churchill, Roosevelt, de Gaulle, Lenin, Hitler, Huey Long, Mahatma Gandhi, Fidel Castro. As the list of names suggests, an inspiring leader may be a demagogue or a statesman; but he has an unusual capacity for transmitting to his followers a sense that he pursues grandiose goals, more lofty than mere self-interest, and is worthy of admiration, awe, imitation, and obedience.

3. *Legality.* In this case legitimacy rests on a belief that power is wielded in a way that is legal; the constitutional rules, the laws and the powers of officials are accepted as binding because they are legal; what is done legally is regarded as legitimate. Weber believed that legality was the usual basis of legitimacy in the modern era, but he might have revised his opinion if he had lived to witness the rise of revolutionary and nationalist leaders in Europe, Asia, Africa, and Latin America. Nonetheless, in much of the modern world and in many different kinds of organizations, it is true that laws, rules, and constitutional practices acquire their legitimacy in large part be-

[4] Max Weber, *The Theory of Social and Economic Organization,* trans. by A. M. Henderson and Talcott Parsons (New York: Oxford University Press, 1947), p. 328.

Political Systems: Differences

cause the process by which they are enacted is assumed to be legal. Whenever legality is the basis for legitimacy, leaders who are known to act illegally are discredited and lose their authority.

To each of these three main grounds for legitimacy, then, there corresponds a "pure" form of authority: (1) traditional authority, (2) "charismatic" authority, from a Greek word used by early Christians meaning "the gift of grace," and (3) legal authority.[5]

Weber recognized that these "pure" forms were abstractions or, as he called them, "ideal types." In an actual political system one might encounter all three kinds of legitimate authority—as, indeed, our choice of examples has already suggested would be true in the American national government.

Like Aristotle, Weber also sought to show how one kind of authority might change into another. The Presidency of Franklin D. Roosevelt can be used to illustrate Weber's ideas. The traditional authority attached to the Presidency was expanded by Franklin D. Roosevelt who had an immense popular following; Weber would have called Roosevelt a "charismatic" leader. Then, when Roosevelt's reform proposals were enacted into law, "bureaucracies" (as Weber would call them) were created to administer the new laws—as in the case of the National Labor Relations Act, the Social Security Act, and the like. Thus Roosevelt's *charismatic* authority enabled him to break through the *traditional* limits on the authority of the Chief Executive, which, in turn, was transformed into *legal* authority. Weber believed that charismatic authority was inherently unstable, and tended to be transformed by subordinates and successors to the inspirational leader into either traditional or legal authority. Both these forms of authority, he held, were more enduring, since they did not depend on the existence of a particular leader who possessed "charisma."

There are obviously some important differences between Aristotle's scheme and Weber's. For one thing Weber dealt only with authority—that is, with legitimate power. His scheme does not concern itself at all with illegitimate regimes. Weber justified his concentration on legitimate governments on the ground that every system of authority "attempts to establish and to cultivate belief in its legitimacy," an observation about political systems that we have already encountered in the preceding chapter.

In the second place, unlike Aristotle, Weber did not distinguish political systems according to their moral value. To Weber, even legitimacy was a purely empirical concept; the test of legitimacy was what the members of the political system thought of their leaders, not what Weber or someone else thought. The fact that a leader's power was legitimate did not, to Weber, make that system good.

Curiously enough, Weber has been criticized both for omitting standards of evaluation and for including them. Some critics have interpreted him as saying that all legitimate governments are good—and equally good. Yet on

[5] A puzzling feature of Weber's general theoretical scheme arises from the profusion of classification schemes in his unfinished work *Wirtschaft und Gessellschaft*. These schemes are based on the application of essentially the same criteria to a number of different aspects of the social system; sometimes, however, there appear to be four main criteria and sometimes only three. Evidently, by the time he came to discuss the basis of legitimacy in the final sections of his volume, he had dismissed the fourth of these; had he employed it, one might have expected an analysis of a system of authority based on the acceptance of an absolute standard of value.

any scrupulous reading of Weber it seems clear that he harbored no such attitude. He intended his categories to be neutral, descriptive, and scientific rather than ethical or "normative." Unlike Aristotle, he sought to exclude any criterion that would depend either on his own moral evaluations of different forms of authority or on an appeal to specific standards of value that he might expect his reader to share. Some critics have attacked Weber precisely because he did seek to be "value-free" and "scientific." The dispute over the proper or inherent place of values in such political analysis has received so much attention from political theorists in recent years that we shall want to devote a good deal more time to it, as we shall do so in the last chapter.

Even as a scientific classification, however, Weber's typology seems deficient, since it makes no place for a number of distinctions that most students of politics would regard as interesting and significant. For example, his scheme does not distinguish a stable democracy from a stable monarchy, for both *could* contain about the same mixture of traditional, charismatic, and legal authority. In Weber's defense, it might be said that he was less concerned with political systems than with the various types of authority, and "pure" types at that. But some significant kinds of authority also seem to be missing from Weber's scheme, or else several different forms of authority are confounded under the same heading. Where, for example, would one locate the authority of the expert? An expert's authority is not necessarily grounded on an appeal to legality, and ordinarily it is neither traditional nor charismatic.

Concrete Systems and Abstract Classifications

The ways of distinguishing political systems proposed by Aristotle and Weber both have drawbacks as well as advantages. As we stressed at the outset, this is likely to be true of any system of classification. To repeat what was said at the beginning of this chapter, there is no one best classification scheme for political systems. How useful any given scheme is depends on one's purposes.

A classification is a way of simplifying—and, in this sense, "distorting" reality. All empirical analysis requires some simplifying "distortion." If every atom were treated as unique, physics would be impossible; if every medical case were considered unique, no advances in medicine could occur. In empirical analysis knowledge consists of generalization, which requires one to exclude the unique in favor of the general properties of a concrete event or system.

In the real world, concrete systems rarely represent "pure" types; they are usually *mixed.* This is true in physics, biology, medicine and, of course, politics. No matter what scheme of political classification one might propose, it would be difficult to find concrete systems that exhibited only the characteristics used in that scheme. Consider any national political system, that of the United States, for example. In some respects the American system is democratic. We have frequent elections, widespread suffrage, competing political parties, peaceful assumption of office by winning candidates, and so on. But some aspects of the system, such as the postal department or the military, are hierarchical, or, one might say, monocratic. In the relations among leaders in the executive branch, Congress, the political parties, and private organizations, there is also an element of bargaining. Consequently, **30** when one classifies the American political system as a democratic system, he necessarily abstracts one aspect of the system out of the concrete reality. It could also be classified as a bargaining system or, for certain purposes, even as a hierarchy.

Despite these inherent difficulties, in any method of classifying concrete objects some criteria are usually related more closely than others to a wide range of phenomena. In politics, three differences among political systems are closely related to a wide variety of other aspects of a system. If systems differ in one or more of these ways, they are likely to differ in a great many other ways as well. These three important differences are:

1. The extent to which the government is legitimate and the power of leaders is accepted as authority.
2. The proportion of the members who influence the decisions of the government.
3. The number of sub-systems and the amount of independence they have.

We shall briefly consider each of these differences.

Legitimacy and Authority

Weber, we saw, concerned himself primarily with legitimate governments. Yet political systems evidently vary a great deal in the extent to which their members regard their governments as legitimate; officials and other leaders vary a great deal, from one political system to the next, in the extent to which they rely on naked power or on authority.

How do leaders win compliance for their policies? A leader has certain resources at his disposal—money, police, privileges, weapons, status, and so on. He can use these resources to obtain compliance for his policies. Suppose a leader wished to enforce a policy requiring all peasants to give up their land-holdings and enter collective farms. He could use his resources to increase the rewards for those who comply or to increase the disadvantages to those who failed to comply. Thus he could act in one or more of four ways:

To encourage compliance, he could	*To discourage non-compliance he could*
1. Increase rewards for complying.	3. Decrease rewards from other alternatives.
2. Decrease disadvantages of complying.	4. Increase disadvantages of other alternatives.

Now during any brief period, the more of his resources he uses to secure compliance for one policy, the less he has available for securing compliance with other policies. In general, then, leaders have some interest in economizing on their political resources. Resources are not, in any case, limitless.

Individuals have internal sources of rewards and deprivations as well as external sources. Examples of internalized rewards are the feeling that one has done a good job, followed the dictates of conscience, done what is right, performed one's duty, and so forth; conversely, internalized penalties include the feeling that one has done a bad job, violated one's conscience, committed an evil act, and so on. Now from a leader's point of view, the more that citizens comply with policies because of internal rewards and deprivations, the less resources he needs to allocate to create external rewards and deprivations. If a leader could win compliance for his policies simply by transmitting information as to what he wanted citizens to do, with no external rewards or deprivations whatsoever, securing compliance would be all but costless.

When a political system is widely accepted by its members as legitimate, and when the policies of its officials and other leaders are regarded as morally binding by citizens, then the costs of compliance are low. Conversely, when legitimacy and authority are low, leaders must use more of their money, police, privileges, weapons, status, and other political resources to secure compliance.

Popular governments—democracies—necessarily require more legitimacy and authority than dictatorships. Political leaders cannot impose a democracy on a people if a majority (or even, in practice, a very large minority) reject democracy as an illegitimate system. Policies that lack authority, like Prohibition in the United States, generally cannot be enforced by naked power. A chief executive would have needed such a great array of coercive power to enforce Prohibition as to constitute a threat to the system itself. In general, then, in democracies political leaders need authority because they are not permitted to acquire sufficient resources to enforce their policies through naked power.

The Distribution of Political Resources and Influence

In the last chapter, we concluded that in all political systems:
1. Control over political resources is distributed unevenly.
2. Political influence is distributed unevenly.

But to say that political resources and influence are distributed unevenly in every society is by no means the same thing as saying that they are distributed *in the same way* in every society. In fact, the distribution of political resources and influences is, as Aristotle pointed out, an important difference among political systems.

The way in which political resources are distributed to various members of a political system can differ in two important respects. First, the *degree* of inequality in control over political resources is not the same in every system. For example, the fact that the United States had an open frontier during the nineteenth century meant that the ownership of landed property was widely diffused as compared with, say, Russia or China. Income, too, may be distributed with a greater or lesser approximation to equality. Figure 3 illustrates the difference between a perfectly equal distribution of incomes and the way in which incomes were distributed in 1929 in the United States, in 1956, and in "Ruritania." Evidently, the distribution of income was somewhat less unequal in the United States in 1956 than it was in 1929. By comparison, in "Ruritania," where the distribution of income is roughly similar to that in most Latin American, Asian, and African countries, the inequality of income is far more severe.

What is true of wealth and income holds for other political resources as well. Extensive educational opportunities diffuse knowledge widely; restrictions on education limit it to a few. A person's social standing may be something that is unalterably assigned at birth in a rigidly hierarchical way; or, instead, it may be gained by a wide variety of achievements. And so on.

In the second place, societies differ in the extent to which inequalities in political resources are cumulative. Some societies are marked by a pattern

Political Systems: Differences

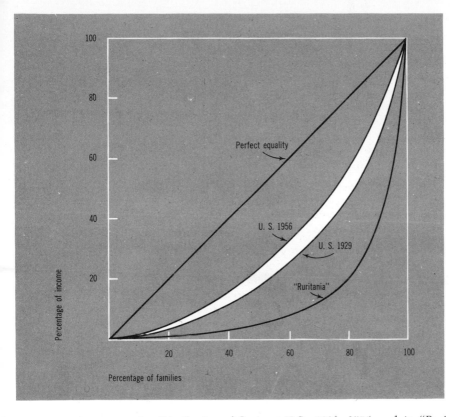

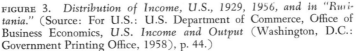

FIGURE 3. *Distribution of Income, U.S., 1929, 1956, and in "Ruritania."* (Source: For U.S.: U.S. Department of Commerce, Office of Business Economics, *U.S. Income and Output* (Washington, D.C.: Government Printing Office, 1958), p. 44.)

of cumulative inequality, where greater control over one resource, such as wealth, is closely related to greater control over most other resources, such as knowledge, social standing, military prowess, and the like. Other societies have a very different pattern: inequalities tend to be non-cumulative. That is, people who are badly off with respect to one resource may make up for it by their control over other resources. Feudalism is an example of cumulative inequality; modern America is an example of non-cumulative inequalities. For example, in many American cities, upper-class, well-to-do Protestants of early American stock lack one important political asset—namely, ethnic solidarity with the great bulk of the voters. Although Fiorello LaGuardia, the famous New York mayor (1934–1945), had neither wealth nor high social origins, he had two assets of inestimable value in New York that Rockefellers and Vanderbilts could not acquire—an Italian father and a Jewish mother.

Differences in degree and the pattern of inequality in the distribution of resources help to account for differences in the extent to which individuals can influence governmental decisions. Where political resources are heavily concentrated in the hands of a single, unified elite, the prospects for popular government are low whereas the likelihood of some form of hierarchical rule **33** is high. Conversely, the chances for popular government are increased if inequalities in resources are reduced or if the pattern of inequality is non-cumulative. (We take up this point in more detail in Chapter 7.)

Although the proposition that political influence is distributed unevenly in all political systems seems to be true, as we concluded in the last chapter, it is often confused with a proposition that is almost certainly false. This proposition, *the ruling elite hypothesis,* is associated with the names of two modern Italians (Vilfredo Pareto and Gaetano Mosca) and a Swiss (Robert Michels), all of whom achieved a measure of acclaim among social theorists disillusioned or cynical about democracy. Although they did not always express their hypothesis clearly, they appear to assert that:

> In every political system there exists a unified minority of members whose choices on matters of government policies, rules, and decisions regularly prevail over the choices of other groups, minorities, coalitions, or majorities in the system. (The Ruling Elite Hypothesis.)[6]

This hypothesis evidently gains plausibility because many people fail to distinguish the existence of a ruling elite from inequality of power. But the two things are not strictly equivalent—any more than (I) "The President has more influence over Congress than anyone else," is equivalent to (II) "The President, and only the President, can always get Congress to do what he wants." If (II) were true, then, of course (I) would necessarily be true; but the converse does not hold: (I) might be true and (II) could be false. In fact, although (I) probably is true, (II) is obviously false, for as everyone knows, in spite of his very great influence the President cannot always win a majority in both Houses for his policies.

There are many circumstances, too, in which individuals who have the greatest power in a political system are nevertheless not a ruling elite. Three of the most common reasons are:

1. Powerful individuals or groups may *disagree* among themselves. In modern democracies some conflict among leaders is guaranteed by the existence of competing political parties which oppose one another in trying to win elections and thus gain control over the government. To prevent the emergence of a ruling elite is, indeed, one reason why those who believe in democracy advocate a system of two or more parties.

2. The power of different leaders may be *specialized.* The price one must pay to acquire power in one sphere is, often, to forego it in another. Sometimes power is deliberately specialized; in modern constitutional systems, for example, leaders of the military or the police are usually prevented by constitutional doctrine or political practice from acquiring extensive power outside their legitimate sphere because of fears that they might use their power to subvert the regime. Specialized power also arises from practical necessity—from limitations imposed by time, knowledge, and abilities. In the United States Congress a committee chairman usually has considerable influence on legislative matters within the jurisdiction of his committee, but often he has very little influence on more remote questions; he simply does not

[6] The hypothesis is perhaps most clearly stated by Vilfredo Pareto in *The Mind and Society* (1916), 4 Vols. (New York: Harcourt Brace, 1935), in Vol. 4, p. 1569. See also Robert Michels, *Political Parties* (1911) (Glencoe, Ill.: The Free Press, 1949), p. 401; and Gaetano Mosca, *The Ruling Class,* Livingston, ed. (New York: McGraw-Hill, 1939), *passim.*

Political Systems: Differences

have the time, knowledge or ability to build up support on matters that lie outside the jurisdiction of his committee.

3. There is strength in numbers. A single timber wolf will stay out of the path of a grizzly bear; but the bear had better not tangle with a pack of wolves. By definition, any one leader in a political system has more power over decisions than any single non-leader. But *in the aggregate,* the power of the non-leaders may exceed that of the leaders. Thus in democracies an elected leader whose influence on an election is far greater than that of any individual voter is often turned out of office despite his best efforts, because the *aggregate* power of a majority of voters to determine who shall hold office is greater than that of any one leader or perhaps even any set of leaders.

The ruling elite hypothesis asserts, in effect, that since political influence is unevenly distributed in all political systems, there are no significant differences in the way political influence is distributed among members of political systems. This is an obvious case of throwing out the baby with the bath water. Imagine for a moment that the amount of each individual's influence could be expressed by a number (as we can if we discuss the distribution of land, income, or wealth). One extreme distribution would be perfect equality of influence, illustrated by the single vertical bar in Fig. 4. Another extreme would be a complete monopoly of political influence by one individual or group, as illustrated in Fig. 5. The ruling elite hypothesis implies that all political systems are rather like Fig. 5. But in practice, the distribution of political influence seems to lie always between these two extremes; the number of possible distributions is endless; and it is reasonable to conclude that the number of different distributions that actually exist or have existed is very great. Figure 6 suggests two quite plausible distributions, which are labelled dictatorship and popular government.

The Independence of Sub-Systems

As we have seen, individuals do not ordinarily belong only to a single political system. An American citizen who lives in Chicago is a member of the political systems of the United States, Illinois, Cook County, and Chicago. He is almost certainly a member of many other political systems, too—a school district, for example, a business firm, a trade union, a church, a lodge, a political party. This multiplicity of memberships is also characteristic of a citizen of the Soviet Union; a Soviet citizen living in Moscow would be a member of the political systems of the city of Moscow, the Russian Soviet Federated Socialist Republic, perhaps an industrial firm, trade union or professional organization, the Communist party, a military unit, and so on. A large modern industrial society could not function as it does without a multiplicity of political systems.

But political systems vary a great deal in the extent to which various sub-systems within their boundaries enjoy autonomy. The extremes can be illustrated by feudalism and modern totalitarianism. European feudal monarchs from the tenth to the thirteenth century had very limited power over the semi-autonomous feudal lords within their kingdoms. The feudal barons, not the king, ruled in their own domains. Within his manor, a baron raised his own military force, enforced law and order, coined money, and regulated

35

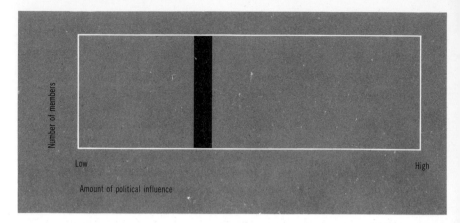

FIGURE 4.   *Equality of Political Influence*

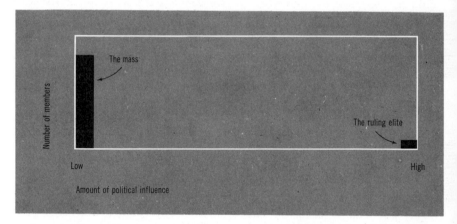

FIGURE 5.   *Monopoly of Political Influence*

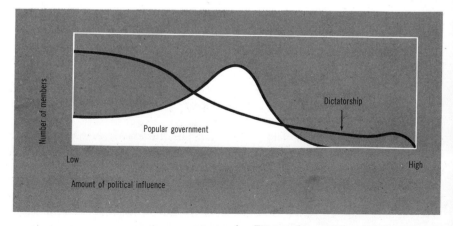

FIGURE 6.   *Dictatorship and Popular Government*

Political Systems: Differences

trade. At the other extreme, modern totalitarian regimes seek to make every political sub-system an agent of the dictatorship; local and regional governments, industry, trade unions, professional associations, youth groups, party units are subordinated to the control of the dictatorship. Although in practice democracies tend to allow a good deal of autonomy to sub-systems, they too vary a good deal. Some democracies—Switzerland, the United States, Canada, and Australia, for example—are federal: their cantons, states, or provinces enjoy a considerable measure of autonomy as a matter of constitutional right. Other democracies—Britain, Denmark, Norway, Sweden, and France, for example—are "unitary": the powers and duties of cities and provinces can be legally determined by the national government. However, the distinction between "federal" and "unitary" systems can easily be exaggerated, for the national government in a "unitary" democracy could not and would not destroy the autonomy that the sub-units of the national government enjoy in *practice*; in all likelihood national leaders who had both the power and the will to destroy local autonomy would also destroy democracy in the process.

In practice, too, in all countries where popular governments have thrived, a great variety of associations have enjoyed considerable autonomy—political parties, trade unions, churches, lobbies, pressure groups, and the like. Thus whether "federal" or "unitary" in legal theory, modern democracies tend to be "federal"—i.e., pluralistic, in actual practice.

Classifications of Political Systems: Summary

It is easy to see, then, how political systems might be classified in many different ways. For example, if we take the three important kinds of differences we have just been considering, we arrive at a formal scheme for classifying political systems.

This classification provides for sixteen different categories instead of the usual three or six (Table 1). When we locate a political system in one of these categories, we have already said a good deal about it; we are in a position to infer a good deal more, or at the very least to expect the appearance of some phenomena rather than others. For example, if a government of "the many"—a democracy—is pluralistic and its legitimacy is weak, we would also expect it to encounter great difficulties in settling conflicts among the various sub-systems; we might reasonably expect such a system to be relatively unstable. In a unitary hierarchy with strong legitimacy, one would expect to find very great conformity and consensus on political matters, both because of the legitimacy of government and the absence of sub-systems around which competing loyalties would be formed. Of course, expectations of this kind would be merely plausible inferences; one could not determine from the classification scheme whether or not they were actually true. In short, the scheme helps to generate hypotheses about political systems, but it cannot confirm or disprove these hypotheses. For example, Aristotle's hypothesis that rule by the many really means rule by the poor can only be settled by empirical inquiry, not by definition.

It should never be forgotten, however, that how we distinguish political systems and how we classify them logically depends on whatever it is we are most interested in. To the extent that what we are interested in varies, our distinctions are also going to vary. Hence no scheme of classification is likely to be satisfactory for all purposes.

	Government Has Strong Legitimacy (Legitimate Systems)		Government Has Weak Legitimacy (Tyrannies)	
	Sub-system Autonomy:		Sub-system Autonomy	
"Final" power over decisions of government exercised by:	Low (unitary)	High (pluralistic)	Low (unitary)	High (pluralistic)
One				
Few				
Many				
Mixed				

Power
and Influence

Power and influence are, as we have seen,
concepts of key importance in political analysis.
Curiously enough, however, systematic analysis of these
concepts is rather recent, partly because serious attempts have
not been made until quite recently to formulate them
rigorously enough for systematic study.
In fact, you may have noticed that so far we have used
the two terms without trying to define them.
But since confused thinking about

the nature of power and influence has been the source of innumerable difficulties to political observers, we cannot postpone that task any longer. A careful examination of the notion of power and the related concept of influence will help a person avoid some widespread traps in political analysis that even highly sophisticated observers often fall into.

One word of warning. The ideas in this chapter are essentially quite simple; they rest on ordinary, everyday common sense. Nonetheless, this chapter requires close reading. For the concepts of influence and power are full of logical traps, and most people—including many people who write about politics—are not accustomed to thinking logically about power and influence. The aim of this chapter is to show you certain common pitfalls in political analysis, so that hereafter you can proceed on your own through a jungle of logic that will be impenetrable only to those who do not have a good map in their minds as they set out.

Influence

Suppose you were to stand on a street corner and say to yourself, "I command all automobile drivers on this street to drive on the right-hand side of the road"; suppose also that all the drivers actually did as you "commanded" them to do. Still, most people would regard you as mentally ill if you were to insist that you had just shown enough influence over automobile drivers to compel them to use the right-hand side of the road. On the other hand, suppose a policeman is standing in the middle of an intersection at which most traffic ordinarily moves ahead; he orders all traffic to turn right or left; the traffic moves right or left as he orders it to do. Then common sense suggests that the policeman acting in this particular role evidently influences automobile drivers to turn right or left rather than go ahead.

Our common-sense notion, then, goes something like this: A influences B to the extent that he gets B to do something that B would not otherwise do. An influence relation between two actors might be illustrated in this fashion:

| A | doesn't influence | B | does | x |
| A | influences | B | doesn't do / does | x / y |

Influence, then, is a *relation*—among individuals, groups, associations, organizations, states. We can use a convenient bit of jargon and say that influence is a *relation among actors* in which one actor induces other actors to act in some way they would not otherwise act. Of course this definition also includes instances in which actor A induces B to go on doing something he is now doing, though B would stop doing it except for A's inducements.

In principle, then, we can determine the *existence* of influence, and also the *direction* of influence: who influences whom. In practice it is often difficult to find out who influences whom, but we shall postpone considering the practical obstacles in order to deal with a preliminary conceptual problem. Often it is not enough to know simply that some actors influence others. Frequently one also wants to know what the *relative* influence is among different actors. Is Thompson more influential with the mayor than Green is? Who are the most influential people in town on school appropriations? What senators have the most influence in Congress on matters of foreign policy? What countries are the most influential on disarmament questions in the United Nations? Which actors are the least influential in these situations? In the United States are poor people generally less influential on questions of taxation than rich people? In short, one wants to know *how much* influence actor A has over actor B, and one wants to *compare* the amount of influence different actors have over others.

One would find it almost impossible to discuss political life without comparing the influence of different actors. Even to distinguish a democracy from a dictatorship requires one to estimate the relative influence of citizens and leaders. Aristotle's famous classifications scheme obviously assumes that one can measure—and thus compare—relative amounts of influence; for in order to classify any particular political system one must first determine who has the most influence in the system—one person, a few, or a majority?

However, attempts to compare the relative influence of different actors in a political system are the source of great confusion in political analysis. Probably the most important cause of confusion is the fact that many different measures of influence are used, and they are almost always used implicitly rather than explicitly. It is as if two neighbors, one very tall and the other very short, each paced off the length of the boundary between their properties and fell to arguing over the results without ever noticing that one of them took long steps while the other took short steps. To reduce this kind of fruitless controversy, let us consider some of the underlying measures of influence that are used—usually implicitly—to compare the relative influence of different actors.

FIVE WAYS OF COMPARING INFLUENCE

It will help if we pause to take another look at our common-sense definition of influence: A influences B to the extent that A gets B to do something that B would not otherwise do. Somehow, then, A changes B's behavior from what it would have been. If so, why not measure A's influence by the *extent or amount of the change* in B's behavior from what it would have been? The first three underlying measures of influence we are going to examine all rest on this simple idea: The greater the change in some aspect of B's inner or overt behavior that A induces, the greater A's influence over B.

This way of thinking about influence is analogous to the concept of force in mechanics. In mechanics object A exerts a force on object B if A produces a change in the velocity of B. Galileo's famous law of inertia states that a body left to itself will move with uniform velocity in one and the same direction. Any change in the velocity of a body, then, indicates the presence of a force. And the size of the force is proportional to the size of the change in velocity. Thus one object exerts more force than another on a third if the first produces a greater change in velocity.

Although we ought not to push such analogies very far, there is little doubt that our ideas about underlying measures of influence rest on intuitive notions very similar to those on which the idea of force rests in mechanics. The underlying idea in both cases can be represented in the following way: 41

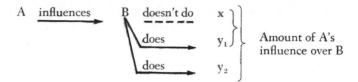

Since the change represented by the vector from x to y_1 is less than the change represented by the vector from x to y_2, A's influence over B is greater in the second case than in the first.

Let us now turn to some underlying measures of influence that draw on this idea.

1. *The amount of change in the position of the actor influenced.* Here is a typical statement illustrating this way of comparing influence:

> Considering what our foreign policy was when Truman came into office and what it was when he left, it is fair to conclude that no other President has ever exerted so much influence over Congress on foreign policy actions in times of peace. Joining the UN, Greek-Turkish Aid, the Marshall Plan, creating and joining NATO—these all represented profound innovations and great breaks with the past.

Now consider the following example:

Members of a school board are debating the question of raising teachers' salaries. One member, A, wants to keep salaries as they are. B would like to raise salaries by $250 a year, C favors an increase of $500, and D wants to add $1,000. The four members of the board can be visualized standing along a chalk line according to the amount of salary increase each one favors:

A	B	C	D
$0	$250	$500	$1,000

Two other citizens, Thompson and Green, would like the board to adopt D's position:

> *Thompson:* I know I can't budge either A or C, but I can get B to join C and accept a $500 increase. B gets a lot of business from me. I know from past experience with him that he'll be willing to compromise on that figure if I ask him to; but I'm sure if I try to push him beyond $500 he'll get stubborn and I won't get anywhere.

> *Green:* Well, I know from past experience that I can't budge C either. I just don't have any influence with C at all. But I can get both A and B to agree to $500.

> *Thompson:* Well, Green, you evidently have more influence with A than I do. We both seem to have the same amount of influence with B, and neither of us has any influence over C.

If Green and Thompson were accurate in their initial estimates, one would be inclined to agree with Thompson's conclusion. In this case as in many others when we say that one actor has "more" influence than another over some third actor, we mean that the one is capable of producing a greater change in the position held by the third.

However, it is not always satisfactory or even possible to measure the relative influence of different political actors in this way. For one thing, we do not always know what the initial positions of the different actors were, nor how much they have actually changed. In politics, individuals sometimes take extreme positions for bargaining purposes, hoping in this way to end up with a compromise that is very close or even identical to their real but concealed initial position. In fact, one of the most important skills in politics— one of the reasons why the practice of politics is an art—is the ability to detect a bargaining position and to guess correctly how much it diverges from the adversary's "real" position. Another skill is just the converse: the capacity to conceal one's real position and create belief in one's bargaining position. In international politics and labor-management disputes, parties often try to mask their real positions by threats, bluffs, and displays of strength—troop movements, angry words, strike-votes. The need to uncover an adversary's true position in turn leads to intelligence operations, research, espionage, and attempts to test his intentions by counter-threats and counter-moves.

Moreover, it is not always possible to decide whether a change in position is larger or smaller than another change. In the case of the school board, if A changes to B's position and C to D's, which change would be the larger? It is true that A's change involves less money, but perhaps A places a much higher value on being economical than C does; he may be much more reluctant to shift to B's position than C is to shift to D's position. In this sense it is reasonable to say that it takes more influence to induce A to vote for a $250 increase than B to vote for a $500 increase. What we need, in short, is a measure of what might be called the psychological distance involved in a change. This suggests a second underlying measure of influence.

2. *The subjective psychological costs of compliance.* Here are some typical statements embodying this measure of influence:

The influence of the old-fashioned political boss declined as immigrant groups became assimilated into American life and as social security took over many of the functions of the boss, for the boss's followers had less and less need, or desire, for his services—the basket of food at Thanksgiving and Christmas, intervening with the police, the stray job with the city, and so on.

It doesn't take a President with much influence to get support for welfare measures among congressmen from urban areas, because they are already in favor of it. It takes a lot more influence to get congressmen from rural districts in the Midwest to go along.

These statements point up the fact that a seemingly equal change in the "objective" positions of two different actors may actually require quite different amounts of subjective change. The "costs" of complying with the wishes of someone else can be very different for different people, depending on their values and their situation.

For example, consider different members of a labor union faced with the prospect of a strike. Some members, let us say, have managed to put aside savings in anticipation of the strike; others have not. A union leader who has enough influence to persuade the first group to vote for a strike may very well not have enough influence to persuade the second group. To the members who have no savings, the "costs" of a strike are likely to seem much higher than to the members who do. Hence it takes correspondingly greater influence to persuade the second group to strike.

In the same way, it takes more influence to induce pacifists to support the draft than militarists; isolationists to support the UN than internation-

43

alists; southern Democrats rather than northern Democrats to support civil rights legislation.

In practice, to be sure, this underlying measure cannot always be applied, since we do not always know what the differences are in the real psychological costs of compliance among different individuals. Nevertheless, one often makes guesses based on known difference in values and situation; and there is no doubt that a good deal of confusion about relative influence might be avoided if the assumptions concerning subjective costs were perfectly clear.

3. *The amount of difference in the probability of compliance.* Consider again the hypothetical case in which you stand on the edge of a busy street in an American city and silently "command" all the automobile drivers to drive on the right. To use the fact that the drivers did indeed drive on the right as evidence for your influence would, it was suggested, make you a likely candidate for a mental institution. For everyone knows that whether or not you "command" them to do so, in this country drivers are compelled by law to drive on the right and would do so without your "command." In other words, the chances that any given driver will drive on the right are already very high—say 999 out of 1,000, allowing for the rare deviant case; and your silent "command" does not alter these chances in the slightest. The policeman, however, is in a different position. Perhaps if he were not standing there only 1 car out of 10 would turn right at that particular intersection. But on his signal, every car turns right. In your case the difference in the probability that they will turn right when you "command" them to do so, and when you don't "command" them to do so, is exactly zero. With the policeman, the change is from 1 chance out of 10 to 10 out of 10—a difference of nine chances out of ten.

Why not measure relative influence, then, by the size of the difference in probabilities of compliance? Notice that the *difference* in probabilities is what matters. If 59 out of 60 Democratic senators vote for a bill proposed by a Democratic President, it would be premature to conclude that the President has great influence with his Congressional party. What we must know first is how many Democratic senators would have voted for the measure anyway, even if the President took no position on it at all.

Here is a statement that implies this underlying measure:

With Congressman X, the Farm Bureau Federation has enormous influence, the Chamber of Commerce considerably less, and the AFL–CIO almost none. Over the years, the Farm Bureau has learned that whenever Congressman X is not going to vote for a bill the Bureau wants to pass, all they have to do is to get on the phone and indicate how they stand. The chances are 9 out of 10 that he will vote the way they want him to. In similar circumstances involving business questions the Chamber of Commerce can get him to change about one time out of three. The AFL–CIO, on the other hand, wins him over less than one time out of ten.

The example also illustrates some of the difficulties with this measure. First, well grounded estimates of "chances" or probabilities require either random events, as with a coin or a die, or else a large number of past occurrences of equivalent events. Political decisions are ordinarily neither random nor equivalent. Hence it is usually difficult to estimate probabilities except in a very loose way. Second, it is often difficult to know the initial likelihood of a particular event because, as has already been indicated, the initial positions of various participants are often unknown. Finally, the mere difference in probabilities is not a wholly satisfactory measure precisely because it does not take into account either of the two previous dimensions—the extent of change in position and the costs of compliance.

4. *Differences in the scope of the responses.* Consider a statement like the following:

Taken all in all, the Majority Leader is the most influential man in the Senate. A committee chairman is usually one of the most influential leaders on matters falling within the jurisdiction of his committee, but on other questions he usually wields little more influence than the average member. The Majority Leader, on the other hand, tends to be highly influential on practically any matter that comes before the Senate.

So far in our analysis the responses of those subject to influence have been considered roughly similar and therefore comparable. All actions were assumed to be of approximately the same nature. The decisions of different school-board members on teachers' salaries, for example, are comparable because they all deal with the same subject, teachers' salaries. But can we compare the relative influence of different actors when they are influencing other actors on different kinds of questions? For example, if by any of the three measures already discussed it were found that President Truman was more influential than President Eisenhower on matters of foreign policy, but President Eisenhower was more influential on matters of domestic policy, could we merge these two different kinds of issue into a single common "scope" and thus decide which of the two presidents was the more influential with Congress over the whole scope of congressional action?

This is a troublesome problem. No wholly satisfactory solution to it has yet been found. Meanwhile, however, it is possible to avoid some snares that observers frequently fall into when they have tried to analyze influence.

First, a statement about influence that does not clearly indicate the scope it refers to verges on the meaningless. When one hears or reads that X is highly influential, the proper question is: "Influential with respect to what?" The failure to insist on this simple question often leads political observers astray. For example, some studies of American cities report the existence of a "dominant" elite that "runs" the city. Thus in "Regional City," a large southern city, 14 well-informed persons were given four lists totaling more than 175 names and were asked to give "their opinions on who were the top leaders on each of the lists." The 10 names on each list most frequently named by the judges were assumed to be "the top leaders." The 40 persons chosen in this way were then described as the "top leaders" in Regional City.[1] Unfortunately, however, these conclusions are all vitiated by the fact that the 14 judges were never asked to specify in what areas of activity different leaders were influential. Are the men who decide on the candidates for mayor the same as those who determine school appropriations? City policies on redevelopment? On segregation and desegregation?

On the evidence presented, it is impossible to know. We simply cannot tell whether men who are influential in Regional City on some questions are or are not influential on other questions. A concern for the scope within

[1] Floyd Hunter, *Community Power Structure* (Chapel Hill: University of North Carolina Press, 1953).

which different leaders exert their influence might have established the exist-ence of a single, homogeneous ruling elite. On the other hand, conceivably it might have led to the discovery of leaders drawn from other social or economic groups. In fact, studies of American communities in which different issue-areas are examined often reveal a highly pluralistic structure.

Second, even when different sectors of influence are clearly designated, it may be difficult or impossible to say which of several actors is the most influential over the whole scope of their influence. An analogous problem arises if we try to compare two athletes who compete in different sports. Was Babe Ruth a better athlete than Jack Dempsey? The question seems unan-swerable. We might measure Babe Ruth against other hitters by using the number of home runs as a measure, and we might measure Dempsey against other fighters by using the number of knockouts, but how to compare home runs with knockouts? If two athletes were to compete in two or more of the same sports, perhaps we could say that one was a better athlete than the other if the one was as good as or better than the other in all fields of compe-tition. For example, if A was as good a hitter as B in baseball, an equally good boxer, but better in squash, we might then say that A was a better athlete than B.

In exactly the same way it seems reasonable to say that one actor is more influential than another over the whole scope of their influence only if A's influence is not less than B's in any particular issue-area and is greater than B's in at least one issue-area. If Green and Thompson are highly influential on issues having to do with the public schools and urban redevelopment, and if Green is more influential than Thompson on political nominations, then Green is more influential than Thompson over the whole scope of their influence.

Real life, however, does not always produce such neatly tailored situa-tions. Green may be more influential than Thompson on school questions, while Thompson may be more influential than Green on political nomina-tions. What do we say in this case? We might try to assign weights to different issue-areas, but weights are bound to be arbitrary. If schools are given a weight of 1, what weight should be given to political nominations—2, 5, ½? How can we justify the weights we assign?

There is at present no single best way of solving the problem of compara-bility when different actors have different levels of influence in several differ-ent issue-areas. Perhaps the most important lesson the student of politics can gain from this is the need for caution and clarity in making comparisons of influence over several issue-areas. As in many other cases, it is wise in political analysis to specify whether we are adding oranges, or apples, or oranges *and* apples.

5. *The number of persons who respond.* If Green controls 5,000 votes and Thompson 10,000, it seems reasonable to say that Thompson has more influence in elections than Green.

To use the number of persons who respond in a certain way as a measure of influence is so obvious and clear that one might suppose it to be flawless. Alas, like other underlying measures this one also has its limitations. These are suggested by the other measures we have already discussed. Green may be able to induce his voters to make a greater change in their positions than Thompson can. Or Green may be able to sway his captive voters even when

Power and Influence

the disadvantages of compliance seem to them very great, whereas Thompson can only get his voters to do things that do not matter much to them anyway. Or Green's control may be much more definite: The likelihood that his captive voters will do what he asks is virtually certain, whereas Thompson's control is much more uncertain. Finally, Green may be able to control his voters over a broader range of issues than Thompson can; Green, perhaps, can deliver his 5,000 votes on any kind of election, local, state, or national, or on any referendum, whereas Thompson can deliver his 10,000 votes merely in local elections.

Summary. All five of the underlying measures of influence we have examined help to illuminate some important aspects of influence. All five have limitations. The analysis suggests the following injunctions to the student of politics:

1. Look for information that will enable you to use as many measures as possible in trying to determine relative influence.

2. Adapt your comparison to the kind of information available.

3. Be specific. A paradigm for any comparison of power might be: "_____ is more influential than _____ with respect to _____ as measured by _____ and _____."

4. Be constantly aware of what you have had to leave out of your appraisal. (In what follows, we shall frequently violate each of these injunctions except this one!)

POTENTIAL INFLUENCE VERSUS ACTUAL INFLUENCE

It is one thing to describe or measure differences in influence, but it is quite another to explain these differences. As we have already seen (Chapter 3), the reasons why some individuals or groups acquire more influence than others over some scope of decisions are reducible to three:

1. Some actors have more political resources at their disposal than others. Or

2. Given the resources at their disposal, some actors use more of them to gain political influence. Or

3. Given the resources at their disposal, some actors use them more skillfully or effectively than others do.

Thus it is important to distinguish between the past or current influence of a particular actor within some scope of decisions, his probable future influence, and his *maximum potential influence* if he were to use *all* his existing political resources with optimum skill to acquire influence within that scope of decisions. An actor's current influence in any given scope always (or nearly always) falls short of his maximum potential influence. Consider the following imaginary case:

Rodney Brown is the richest man in town. In fact, he has made a small fortune on the stock market. He owns a controlling share in the most important local newspaper, he completely owns one radio station, he has a large interest in the biggest bank in town, and he owns dozens of down-town commercial properties. In addition, he has enough investments in gilt-edge securities to insure, as some of his envious fellow citizens put it, that Rodney will never have to put in an honest day's work as long as he lives.

Rodney happens to be deeply interested in only two things: elegant living

47

and the ballet. He lives expensively and he pours his money prodigiously into support for eternally bankrupt ballet companies. He is considerably less interested in politics than in the coddled egg he eats for breakfast every morning. Rodney has few views on local and national affairs, except as these may touch on the ballet, and little influence.

"What with his wealth and all, Rodney has more potential influence on local affairs than anyone in this town," his friends sometimes say dolefully. "And he has a good deal less actual influence than his chauffeur, Woodrow, who happens to be the Democratic precinct leader in Rodney's neighborhood—though Rodney probably doesn't even know it."

Thus Rodney's *potential* influence on local affairs is, at a maximum, obviously high; his *actual* influence is negligible.

Rodney's brother Walter has never had Rodney's flair for outguessing the stock market. He works hard at a job in one of Rodney's radio stations, earns a modest living, and between his job and his family has little time for his great passion—local affairs. Rodney dreams of ballet, Walter dreams of what he could do in local politics if he only had half a chance.

One fine day, Rodney dies suddenly. To everyone's surprise (including Walter's) it turns out that his whole fortune does not, after all, go to that experimental ballet company in New York. It goes to Walter.

As this example illustrates, we cannot infer what the differences in political influence will be among different actors simply from the differences in their access to political resources. In our example:

1. Given his resources, Rodney's potential influence on local affairs was, at a maximum, very much higher than Walter's or Woodrow's influence. But

2. Rodney's actual influence was probably less than his chauffeur's. And

3. With the same resources as Rodney had, Walter's probable future influence is far greater than Rodney's influence was ever likely to be.

Thus an attempt to rank the influence of Rodney, Walter, and Woodrow might look something like this:

Maximum potential influence on local affairs:	Actual influence up to the present:	Expected future influence on local affairs:
1. Rodney	1. Woodrow	1. Walter
2. Walter	2. Walter	2. Woodrow
3. Woodrow	3. Rodney	

Now let us consider an example drawn from military affairs, where the difference between maximum potential military power, present military power, and expected future power is obviously a matter of critical importance. A leading student of international politics has pointed out:

The war potential of a country will be larger than it would be otherwise if, in event of a major war, individuals are motivated, for whatever reason, to forego the satisfaction of personal interests that conflict with the large commitment of resources to waging war. The stronger the motivation, the greater the production of military power from the ecomonic resources and administrative capacity at the disposal of the nation. Motivation for war is strong or high, in contrast to weak or low, depending on whether the configuration of various critical motivations is more or less appropriate to an intense war effort.[2]

[2] Klaus Knorr, *The War Potential of Nations* (Princeton: Princeton University Press, 1956), p. 43.

Power and Influence

In 1939 Germany had considerably more military power in being than did the United States. From 1935–1939 Germany had produced $12 billion worth of combat munitions; the United States had produced $1.5 billion. In mid-1939 Germany had four times as many men under arms as the United States; in 1940 fourteen times as many. In 1939 German munitions output was ten times that of the United States. In 1940 Germany had twice as large an inventory of machine tools as the United States.[3]

The maximum potential military might of the United States was, however, much greater than Germany's, measured by almost any index: population, food supply, raw materials, manufacturing output, production of capital goods. In 1938, for example, the United States produced more than twice as large a share of the world's manufactured goods as Germany, and three times as large a share of capital goods.[4]

In 1939 what could one reasonably expect about the future balance of military power between the two countries? This was more difficult to compare. On the one hand, the United States still had 9 million unemployed who could easily be absorbed in an expanding defense economy. Up to a point, increases in military outlays would be economically rather painless. On the other hand, by tradition, ideology, and culture Americans were distinctly unwarlike. Expenditures for rearmament were widely regarded as a painful necessity at best, and at worst as sheer waste. In 1939 the United States government spent a little more than $1 billion on national defense, or about 1.3 percent of the gross national product.[5] Nazism, by contrast, glorified taut discipline, dictatorship, violence, war, the international power of the Third Reich, the need to sacrifice for the fatherland. Measured by incentives to use their resources for war, then, one might have concluded in 1939 and even in 1941 that although the United States had a greater military potential than the Third Reich, it was reasonable to expect that, in the near future, the balance of actual military power would favor Germany. Pearl Harbor and the humiliating military setbacks of 1942 changed all this. What had been unrewarding sacrifices were now backed by sentiments of patriotism, the need to win a major war, national survival. Given these changes in American incentives, our actual military might rapidly moved closer to our military potential. In 1939, 1 out of every 150 persons in the American labor force was in military service; in 1944, 1 out of 6. By 1944 defense outlays had risen to nearly $90 billion, more than 40 percent of the gross national product.[6]

Thus the influence an actor exerts in some sphere of decisions may fluctuate, *but it rarely approaches his maximum potential influence in that sector.* Why is this so? There seem to be two main reasons. First, only a few actors ever acquire a high degree of political skill. Second, only a few actors ever feel that it is worthwhile to use their resources to the full in order to maximize their political influence in a given sector. We shall return to these limiting factors in the next chapter. Enough has been said, I hope, to indicate how important it is to maintain a clear distinction between an actor's past or present influence, the influence it is reasonable to expect he will exert in the future under certain specified conditions, and his maximum potential influence

---

[3] *Ibid.*, p. 33; Table 1, p. 34; pp. 191, 250.
[4] *Ibid.*, pp. 184, 189.
[5] U.S. Department of Commerce, *U.S. Income and Output* (Washington, D.C.: Government Printing Office, 1958), Table I–1, p. 118.
[6] Knorr, *op. cit.*, p. 250; and *U.S. Income and Output*, Table I–1, p. 119.

It is now easy to see why some individuals seeks to increase their influence by gaining control over the State. For when an actor controls the State, he can enforce his decisions with the help of the State. More concretely, he can use the State's monopoly over physical coercion to try to secure compliance with his policies. But one can seek compliance not only through punishments but also through rewards; and control over the State generally provides resources that can be used to create large benefits as well as severe punishment. In short, the State is a peculiarly important source of *power*. Let us examine this point more closely.

Two kinds of influence are sometimes singled out for particular attention:

1. *Coercive influence:* influence based on the threat or expectation of extremely severe penalties or great losses, particularly physical punishment, torture, imprisonment, and death.

2. *Reliable influence:* influence in which the probability of compliance is very high.

Coercive influence can be illustrated graphically as follows: Imagine a continuum representing various degrees of some value that A regards as important—honor, wealth, prestige, popularity. A's present position is at A_0 on the continuum. That is, a gain in, say, honor, for A is represented by a move to the right; a loss in honor is represented by a move to the left.[7] Hence one might try to influence A by offering him rewards or threatening him with

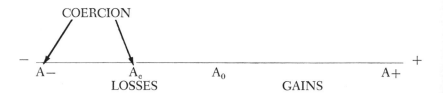

penalties, or some combination of the two. In other words, one might induce A to do something he would not otherwise do by promising to make him better off than he is now ($100 reward if he does), threatening to make him worse off than he is now ($100 fine if he doesn't), or both ($100 reward if he does, $100 fine if he doesn't). The domain of *influence*, one might say, runs all the way from one extreme to the other, from A— to A+ and includes all possible combinations. The extreme left portion of the continuum, let us say from A— to A_c, represents the most severe penalties. This is the domain of *coercive influence*, which is sometimes called *power*.

Exactly what constitutes a "severe" penalty or deprivation is, to be sure, somewhat arbitrary. No doubt what one regards as a severe penalty varies with his experiences, culture, bodily condition, and so on. Nonetheless, whoever can visit severe penalties on others, including imprisonment and death, is bound to be unusually important in any society. Indeed, the State is dis-

[7] Many other terms used to describe this kind of situation can be used interchangeably with gains and losses. Gains are equivalent to rewards, benefits, advantages, inducements, positive incentives, indulgences. Losses are equivalent to penalties, disadvantages, negative incentives, deprivations, sanctions.

Power and Influence

tinguishable from other political systems only to the extent that it successfully upholds its claim to the exclusive right to determine the conditions under which certain kinds of severe penalties, those involving physical coercion, may be legitimately employed.

But very substantial rewards can be made to operate rather like coercion. For if A is offered a very large reward for compliance, then once his expectations are adjusted to this large reward, he suffers a prospective loss if he does not comply. At the extreme ends of the continuum, near A− and near A+, the disadvantages of non-compliance are exceedingly high. In this sense the manipulation of substantial rewards can also be considered "coercive." Negative coercion is based on the threat of extreme punishment, whereas positive coercion is based on the prospect of very large gains. Both negative coercion and positive coercion are sometimes included in the term "power."[8]

The State is, then, a pawn of key importance in struggles over power, for the relatively great resources of the State and its exclusive claim to regulate severe physical coercion means that those who control the State inevitably enjoy great power.

It is one thing to define power and quite another to observe it. How can we actually observe power relations, and particularly how can we determine the relative power of different actors in the real world? In short, with respect to any particular political system how can we answer the question: "Who rules"?

Efforts have been made to study power relations in experimental situations, in laboratories, or in other circumstances in which the observer can pretty well control the situation. Although these efforts are sometimes interesting and useful, obviously they are a long way from real life. We want to know who rules in Jonesville, or Washington, or Moscow, not in a contrived situation. We want to know how power is distributed among the various members of a concrete political system. We need this knowledge before we can go on to other important questions: What kind of a political system is it? How are we to classify it? Do the actors with the most power or the least power come from a particular socio-economic stratum of the community? If so, what stratum? If not, from what strata are they drawn? What are the

---

[8] The existence of both negative and positive coercion is sometimes a source of confusion in political analysis, since writers often either confound the two or ignore positive coercion. A close reading of Harold D. Lasswell and Abraham Kaplan, *Power and Society* (New Haven: Yale University Press, 1950), indicates that they include both negative and positive coercion in their definition of power, though the inclusion of positive coercion is not obvious. They write:

A *decision* is a policy involving severe sanctions (deprivations) . . . *Power* is participation in the making of decisions. . . . It is the threat of sanctions which differentiates power from influence in general. Power is a special case of the exercise of influence: it is the process of affecting policies of others with the help of (actual or threatened) severe deprivations for nonconformity with the policies intended.

Lasswell cites as comparable Locke's use of the term in the *Two Treatises of Government*: "Political Power, then, I take to be a right of making laws, with penalties of death, and consequently all less penalties" (pp. 74–76). These passages appear to suggest that they included only negative sanctions. However, they define "sanctions" to include "reward or punishment by way of any value whatever. The sanction is *positive* when it enhances values for the actor to whom it is applied, *negative* when it deprives him of values" (pp. 48–49).

51

Power and Influence

goals and values of the most powerful actors? The less powerful? How much do these diverge? What changes are taking place in the sources of leadership? In the distribution of power?

Outside the laboratory there are four main ways to observe power relations in order to discern the way in which power is distributed among the members of a political system. Each has advantages and disadvantages. None is perfect. Skillfully used, each can be a highly valuable instrument for inquiry.

First, you can proceed on the assumption that an actor's power is closely correlated with his position in an official or semi-official hierarchy. Who occupies the offices in a political system? Who holds the "major" offices? The minor offices? No offices? What groups are over-represented or under-represented among the officeholders?

The great advantage of this method is its simplicity. Official hierarchies are usually well-defined, the incumbents are clearly designated, records are extensive, information is easily obtainable. The method is particularly useful for detecting large-scale historical changes and gross differences among broad political systems, such as the decline of the landed gentry in English politics and the rise of other socio-economic strata. This method is also helpful in discovering patterns of relationship among different elite groups—how much overlap is there, for example, among occupants of high social positions, high positions in business, high positions in the military, and high positions in politics?

The great weakness of the method, of course, is the shaky assumption on which it rests, for formal position is not necessarily correlated with power. This method would not necessarily uncover the *eminence grise,* the king-maker, the political boss, the confidante; nor would it record the power of a class or stratum that rules indirectly by allotting formal offices to others.

To overcome these defects you can turn to a second method. You can rely on well-placed judges. This was the method used in the study of Regional City and it has been widely imitated. Corrected for the neglect of scope that marred the original study and many others that have followed, this method can be highly useful. It is relatively simple, quick, and economical. The judgments of one set of observers can easily be checked against the judgments of others. The method is useful even in historical studies. It is the recorded judgments of well-placed observers that lead us to Father Joseph, the *Eminence Grise* of Cardinal Richelieu, or to President Wilson's confidante, Colonel House.

The big disadvantage of the method is that it puts us at the mercy of the judges—and how are we to determine who are the best judges? Even seemingly well-placed observers can be misled by false reputations; they may attribute great power where little or none exists. Do we need more judges, then, to judge the judges? Or can we somehow go behind the judgments of the judges and arrive at our own independent appraisal?

The third method is to pierce the façade of formal position and reputation by studying participation in decisions. Which actors actually participate most often in making decisions within this or that scope of activity? Which actors participate in several or many different kinds of activity, and which ones are highly specialized? This method focusses on what people do (or at least what they and others report they do), not on formal office or reputation.

Power and Influence

Moreover, it can help us trace out various patterns of power; we can distinguish power in one issue-area from power in another, general power over many issue-areas from the specialized power of an actor who participates in only one issue-area.

The great disadvantage of this method, however, is that participation or activity is not equivalent to power. A president and his confidential secretary may both participate in all the major governmental decisions of a country, but it would be folly to conclude that they had anything like equal power.

In order to get around this disadvantage, you might try a fourth method. You could weigh the activities of different participants in decisions. You could assign weights by means of some kind of operational definition of one or more of the underlying measures discussed earlier.

One study, for example, reconstructed in considerable detail a set of decisions made over a period of time in New Haven, Conn. From the reconstructed record of various decisions in different issue-areas, the author sought to determine which of the participants had most frequently initiated proposals that were later adopted as actual policy, or had successfully opposed proposals initiated by others. It was assumed that the actors who not only participated in the decisions but were most frequently successful according to these criteria were the most influential.[9] The great advantage of the method is that it uses an operational test, however crude, for appraising the relative power of different participants in decisions, and thus it enables the observer to go behind mere office, reputation, and activity. One disadvantage of the method is the time required to reconstruct decisions in sufficient detail; another is that operational definitions must sometimes be so crude as to lend themselves to serious criticism. For example, which man is the more powerful in a given issue-area: a man who initiates two proposals that are subsequently adopted without objection, a second man who carries through one proposal over very strong initial objections, or a third who initiates 20 policy proposals but succeeds in securing the adoption of only one-third of them?

Every method of detecting and weighing power, then, has decided advantages and disadvantages. None is foolproof. Without commonsense and judgment, all can produce ludicrous results. Used skillfully, however, each is highly useful.

SOME COMMON ERRORS IN THE ANALYSIS OF POWER

It is easy to see why the analysis of power is so full of pitfalls. Here are some common errors that the preceding discussion should help one to detect and avoid:

1. Failing to distinguish clearly between participating in a decision, influencing a decision, and being affected by the consequences of a decision.

2. Failing to identify the scope or scopes within which an actor is said to be powerful.

3. Failing to distinguish different degrees of power, for example, by equating the proposition that power is distributed unequally in a political system with the proposition that the system is ruled by a ruling class.

[9] Robert A. Dahl, *Who Governs?* (New Haven: Yale University Press, 1961).

Power and Influence

4. Confusing an actor's past or present power with his potential power, particularly by assuming that the greater the political resources an actor has access to, the greater his power must be.

5. Equating an actor's expected future power with his potential power, particularly by ignoring differences in incentives and skills.

Political Man

An elementary starting point for all political
theory is the existential fact that members of the human species
live together. With few exceptions human beings do
not carry on their lives in complete isolation. Whatever
may be the elements of instinct, habit, necessity,
or choice that induce people to form societies, man has amply
demonstrated for thousands of years that he is a social
animal. Yet though man is a social animal, neither by
instincts nor by learning is he

necessarily a political animal—at least not in quite the same sense. Even though they live in a society, men need not concern themselves with the politics of that society, nor participate actively in political life, nor cherish the political institutions and values of their society. Some people do, to be sure; but many, as we have seen, do not.

Nonetheless, simply because human beings are social they also develop political systems. Evidently they cannot dwell together without entering into relationships of influence; whenever these relationships become stable and repetitive, political systems exist.

In this looser sense, then, one might say (with Aristotle) that man *is* a political animal. Whatever his own values and concerns as a social being man is inevitably enmeshed in political systems—whether or not he likes or even notices the fact.

However, the individuals who find themselves within the boundaries of a political system are by no means equally concerned with political life. Some people are indifferent to politics, others are more deeply involved. Even among those who are heavily involved in politics, only some actively seek power. And among the power-seekers, some gain more power than the rest.

These four groups—the apolitical strata, the political strata, the power-seekers, and the powerful—can be illustrated in this way:

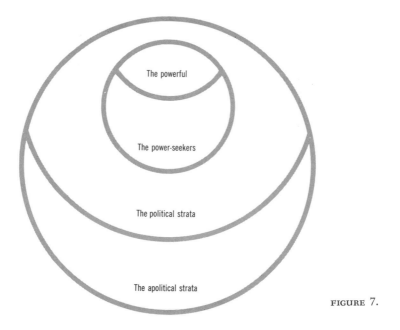

The powerful

The power-seekers

The political strata

The apolitical strata

FIGURE 7.

The Political Strata

The political strata consist of individuals who are psychologically "involved" in governmental decisions. There are various ways in which individuals may be psychologically "involved" in decisions; these different forms of involvement usually run together, but they need not. Four dimensions of involvement in a decision are:

Political Man

1. Interest—how curious one is to know what is happening.
2. Concern—how important one feels the decision is.
3. Information—how much knowledge one has about the decision.
4. Activity—how much one overtly participates in the decision.

In the United States, and probably in most societies, these four dimensions are correlated. For example, a person who has little interest in a presidential campaign and little concern about the outcome of the election is less likely to acquire information about the campaign and the issues involved, and is also less likely to vote in the election itself, than a citizen who has a great deal of interest and concern.[1] Tables 2 and 3 show how interest, concern, and voting turnout were related in the 1956 presidential campaign.

Table 2   RELATION OF DEGREE of Interest in Campaign to Voting Turnout, 1956

| | Degree of Interest in Campaign[a] | | |
	Not Much Interested	Somewhat Interested	Very Much Interested
Voted	58%	72%	87%
Did not vote	42	28	13
	100%	100%	100%
Number of cases	540	695	520

Source: A. Campbell, *et al., The American Voter* (New York: Wiley, 1960), p. 103.
[a] Respondents were classified according to their responses to the following question: "Some people don't pay much attention to the political campaigns. How about you? Would you say that you have been very much interested, somewhat interested, or not much interested in following the political campaigns so far this year?"

Table 3   RELATION OF DEGREE of Concern about Election Outcome to Voting Turnout, 1956

| | Degree of Concern over Election Outcome[a] | | | |
	Don't Care at All	Don't Care Very Much	Care Somewhat	Care Very Much
Voted	52%	69%	76%	84%
Did not vote	48	31	24	16
	100%	100%	100%	100%
Number of cases	230	367	627	459

Source: Ibid., p. 104.
[a] Respondents were classified according to their responses to the following question: "Generally speaking, would you say that you personally care a good deal which party wins the presidential election this fall, or that you don't care very much which party wins?"

Table 4 illustrates the relationship between activity and information in the 1956 election. It is hardly surprising, of course, that those who participated most in the 1956 campaign were more familiar with the issues than those who participated less.

[1] Robert Lane, *Political Life,* 143 ff., and Angus Campbell, *et al., The American Voter* (New York: Wiley, 1960), pp. 101 ff.

Issue Familiarity		Level of Participation		
		Low	Medium	High
High	4	16%	30%	45%
	3	17	27	27
	2	18	19	16
Low	1	49	24	12
		100%	100%	100%
	N	394	770	515

Source: V. O. Key, Jr., *Public Opinion and American Democracy* (New York: Knopf, 1961), Table 8.1, p. 185.

Voting, of course, is only one kind of activity. A study of registered voters in New Haven, Connecticut, included a wide variety of activities in addition to voting—nine having to do with campaigns and elections and four having to do with activities outside campaigns. When both interest and concern were combined into a single measure, the relationship with activity was very strong. As might be expected, citizens who were the most active in local affairs were also likely to be better informed.

Table 5   RELATION BETWEEN ACTIVITY in Local Affairs, Interest, Concern, and Information (New Haven, Conn., 1959)

	Extent of Activity				
	Least	Low	Medium	High	Highest
Highly interested and concerned	16%	27%	47%	64%	72%
Highly informed	20%	17%	21%	39%	62%
Number of cases (total)	188	148	89	68	29

The Apolitical Strata

Because there are several dimensions of involvement, and because each dimension is more or less continuous, the political stratum shades off gradually into the apolitical strata; an exact boundary between the political strata and the apolitical strata must, therefore, be arbitrary. Nonetheless, it is probably true that in most political systems those who display great political interest, concern, information, and activity are not a large proportion of the adults; generally, no doubt, they are a minority. Even in a democratic society the political strata do not include all citizens, for even in democracies a sizeable number of citizens are apathetic about politics and relatively inactive. There are, to be sure, variations from one democracy to another and from time to time; but the existence of political apathy and indifference among many citizens in a democracy seems to be nearly universal. Even the Greek city-states,

Political Man

which are sometimes held up as models of democractic participation (aside from the slaves), were not immune. In Athens, for example, the *demos* was often indifferent. Aristotle wrote of fourth century Athens:

> Payment for attendance at the assembly was, at first, a step which they (i.e., the restored democrats, once more in control after the perturbations at the end of the Peloponnesian War) refused to take. The citizens, however, failed to attend; and the presidents of the assembly were driven to one device after another in order to induce the populace to present themselves for the purpose of ratifying measures. In these circumstances Agyrrhius began by providing an obol a day for attendance: Heraclides . . . increased it to two obols; and Agyrrhius afterward advanced it to three.

By Aristotle's time, citizens received 6 obols a day for attending the Assembly, the town meeting of Athens.[2]

Sometimes, too, New England town meetings are regarded as a model. But just as in Athens, in New England towns many citizens were unconcerned about exercising their rights or fulfilling their political obligations. In New Haven, for example, the problem seems to have been a persistent one. In 1642 the General Court of the Colony "voted that any freeman who after due warning, should fail to appear in the General Courts before the Secretary finished the roll-call, should be fined 1s. 6d; and that any of the rest of the planters who should be absent after their names were read, should be fined one shilling. The novelty of the first few years had worn away, and attendance at the General Courts seemed, to many, burdensome." A century later the problem was still unsolved in New Haven. In 1784 the old colonial town officially became a city, and the first city elections were held. Of some 600 males living in the city, about 250 were excluded as voters either because they could not meet the property requirements or because they had been loyal to Great Britain. Of the 343 eligible males, about one-fourth failed to take the oath and hence could not vote in the first election. Although most of those who were qualified to vote did actually vote for the mayoralty candidates, two days later only about a hundred citizens (out of 261 eligible) showed up to vote for the councilmen.[3]

The problem is still acute today. Only a minority of adult American citizens vote regularly and participate in other ways. In 1950 two well-known pollsters reported the results of a survey of political activities among a cross-section sample of 8,000 adult Americans. The results are shown in Table 6. Except for voting once or more in the preceding four years, only a minority—usually a small minority—of the respondents had engaged in the forms of political activity listed.

Obviously man is not instinctively a political animal. It is true that few people ever live outside a political system; it is also true that by the standards of most of us the benefits of living in political systems far outweigh the disadvantages. Nonetheless, though human beings must and do live in political systems and share the benefits of political life, they do not necessarily participate in political life; they are not necessarily interested in politics, nor do they always care what happens in politics, know much about political events, or

[2] Aristotle, *On the Constitution of Athens*, Appendix IV, in Barker (ed.), *op. cit.*, pp. 379, 383.

[3] Charles H. Levermore, *The Republic of New Haven* (Baltimore: Johns Hopkins University Press, 1886), pp. 44, 231.

Political Man

Table 6   POLITICAL ACTIVITIES OF AMERICAN CITIZENS

Voting
    Once or more in last four years   75%
    Three times or more   47
    Five times or more   21

Discussing public issues with others
    Discusses frequently and takes an equal share in the conversation   21
    Discusses frequently and usually tries to convince others he is right   6

Belonging to organizations that take stands on public issues
    Belongs to one or more such organizations   31
    Belongs to two or more   7

Written or talked to congressman or other public official to give own
    opinion on a public issue
    One or more times in past year   13
    Two or more times in past year   7

Worked for election of a political candidate in last four years   11
Contributed money to a party or candidate in last four years   7

Source: Julian L. Woodward and Elmo Roper, "Political Activity of American Citizens," *The American Political Science Review,* Vol. 44 (December, 1950), pp. 872–885.

share in making decisions. In most political systems, in fact, the political stratum is a minority of the adult population. Moreover, those who are *highly* interested, concerned, informed, and active are an even smaller minority within the political stratum.

Why is it that even in modern societies with widespread education, universal suffrage, and democratic political systems the apolitical stratum is so large? To answer this question would require much more space than can be given here, but a short if somewhat formal answer can be indicated. Essentially there seem to be three reasons why an individual does not become involved in politics.

1. *An individual is unlikely to get involved in politics if he places a low valuation on the rewards to be gained from political involvement relative to the rewards expected from other kinds of human activity.* For many people political activity is a good deal less gratifying than other outlets—family, friends, recreation, and the like. For many, political involvement yields far less affection, income, security, respect, excitement, and other values than working at one's job, watching television, reading, fishing, playing with the children, attending a football game, or assembling a new hi-fi set. For many, the rewards of political involvement are distant and vague, whereas the rewards of other activities are more immediate and concrete. In short, for many people the opportunity costs of political involvement are simply too high to make it worthwhile. These people are unwilling to forego immediate, certain, and concrete benefits or gratifications derived from non-political activities in order to obtain the more remote, uncertain, and abstract benefits that might ensue from political participation.

Just why political involvement is not more rewarding for more people is a question for which no short or easy answer is possible. The explanation, no doubt, turns on the fact that man is not by instinct a reasonable, reasoning civic-minded being. Many of his most imperious desires and the source of many of his most powerful gratifications can be traced to ancient and per-

60

Political Man

sistent biological and physiological drives, needs, and wants. Organized political life arrived late in man's evolution; today man learns how to behave as a political man with the aid and often with the hindrance of instinctive equipment that is the product of a long prior development. To avoid pain, discomfort, and hunger; to satisfy drives for sexual gratification, love, security and respect—these needs are insistent and primordial. The means of satisfying them quickly and concretely generally lie outside political life.

2. *An individual is unlikely to get involved in politics if he thinks that the probability of his influencing the outcome of events, of changing the balance of rewards by means of his political involvement, is low.* Individuals do not engage in activity merely because the *possible* rewards are high, if the *probability* of gaining the rewards is very low. Even though the pay-off to Irish Sweepstakes winners is very high, not everyone buys a ticket, for many people feel that the chance of winning is so slight that they are simply throwing their money away. In the same way, citizens who are pessimistic about their capacity to influence political events may eschew politics on the ground that what they do won't matter anyway. Voters sometimes neglect to vote because they feel that one vote won't change the outcome; citizens often fail to press their views on public officials because they believe that public officials won't pay attention to people like themselves.

Surveys show a strong relationship between a person's sense of political efficacy (the confidence that what one does really matters) and the extent of his political involvement. The weaker one's sense of political efficacy, the less likely one is to become involved. Table 7 is a typical illustration of this relationship. The table shows a strong relation between a sense of political efficacy and voting turnout in the 1956 presidential election. Of those with the highest confidence, 91 per cent voted, compared with only 52 per cent among those with the lowest degree of confidence.

Table 7   RELATION OF SENSE of Political Efficacy to Voting Turnout
in the 1956 Presidential Election

Sense of Political Efficacy

	Low				High
Voted	52%	60%	75%	84%	91%
Did not Vote	48	40	25	16	9
	100%	100%	100%	100%	100%
Number of cases	263	343	461	501	196

Source: Campbell, *et al., op. cit.,* Table 5–6, p. 105.

Figure 8 shows another example. This table shows the relationship among a sample of voters in New Haven between the sense of political efficacy and a general index of local action. The index of local action combines a large variety of campaign, electoral, and non-campaign activities and thus is a more comprehensive measure of political involvement than mere voting.

The confidence one has in one's capacity to be effective in political life depends on many factors. In the United States the sense of efficacy rises with income, social standing, political experience, and, most of all, education. Of course, a person's sense of confidence may also simply reflect a realistic ap-

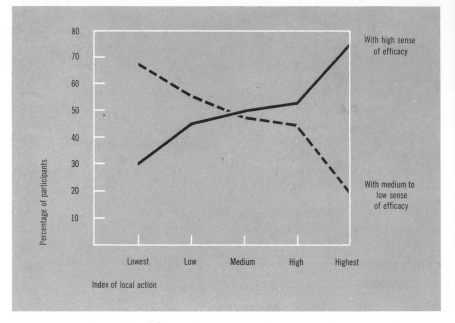

FIGURE 8. *The more a person participates in local affairs, the more likely he is to have a high sense of political efficacy.* (Source: Robert A. Dahl, *Who Governs? Democracy and Power in an American City* (New Haven: Yale University Press, 1961), p. 288.)

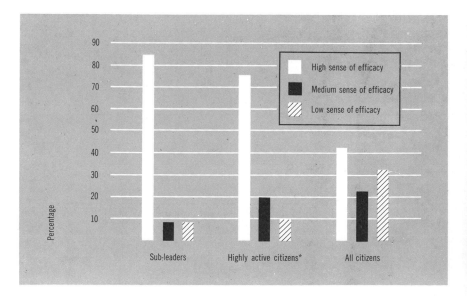

FIGURE 9. *Sub-leaders have a very high sense of political efficacy.* (Source: Dahl, *op. cit.,* p. 289.)

praisal of his influence. Thus it is hardly surprising that among sub-leaders in various political organizations in New Haven, more than 8 out of 10 possess a relatively high sense of efficacy (Fig. 9). Probably one's "personality" has some bearing on one's sense of efficacy. Optimism or pessimism about one's chances of influencing policy is probably related to deeper personality factors, such as an underlying sense of confidence or lack of confidence that pervades a person's entire outlook.

3. *An individual is unlikely to get involved in politics if he believes that the outcome will be relatively satisfactory to him without his involvement.* A citizen who believes that some political decision is important might nevertheless not become involved if he feels quite confident that the decision will turn out well anyway. Just as low confidence in one's political efficacy discourages participation, so high confidence in the all-round justice, legitimacy, stability, and fairness of decisions in one's political system may make one's own participation seem unnecessary. One might expect political involvement to decrease during periods of prosperity and rise during depressions. A comparison of the turnout in United States presidential elections and major periods of depression and prosperity does indeed show some relation; though so many factors influence voting turnout that the results must be interpreted cautiously. However, the percentage of eligible voters who voted in presidential elections climbed to a sharp peak in 1876 during the depression that lasted from 1873–1878. The Greenback Movement and Populism were undoubtedly stimulated by the depressions of 1873–1878 and 1893–1897. The percentage of eligible voters who went to the polls rose during the Great Depression of 1929–1939.

Power-Seekers and Leaders

Within the political strata, some persons seek power much more actively than others. And some persons gain much more power than others. Within the political strata, then, there is a sub-stratum of *power-seekers* and a sub-stratum of powerful *leaders*.

You will notice that what we have just said is a restatement of two propositions set forth in Chapter 3 as empirical characteristics of political systems:

1. Some members of the political system seek to gain influence over the policies, rules, and decisions enforced by the government.

2. Political influence is distributed unevenly among adult members of a political system.

Now to seek power and to gain power are by no means the same thing. Although the two phenomena—seeking power and gaining power—are sometimes confused, clearly they are distinguishable. Not only are some power-seekers unsuccessful in their efforts to gain power; some people who gain power may not actually seek it. This might occur, for example, among those who, like a monarch or a feudal lord, acquire their power by inheritance. In Table 8 the two different dimensions are combined to yield four categories.

We have, then, two important questions: Why do some people seek more power than others? And why do some people gain more power than others?

Table 8   SEEKING POWER AND GAINING POWER

		Extent of Seeking Power	
		Little or No Active Search	Highly Active Search
Extent of power gained	Much	Powerful leaders who do not seek power	Successful power-seekers
	Little or none	Non-leaders who do not seek power	Unsuccessful power-seekers

The Power-Seekers

Every human being has access to resources of some kind. His resources may be pitifully meager—a tiny barren patch of land that barely yields enough food to sustain his life, the labor-time he sells to a landlord for a pittance, a primitive wooden hoe. Or his resources may be enormous and varied—the wealth of a pasha, a famous family name, control over means of communication, a high public position, widespread popularity, a disciplined and loyal band of associates and followers, a far-flung bureaucracy for acquiring intelligence and analyzing information.

These resources could, in principle, nearly always be applied to more than a single purpose. The poor half-starved peasant in his wintry hour of need could burn his wooden hoe in a last desperate struggle to survive; he could use it to club an intruder or drive off an animal; or he and his fellows could use their labor-time and their hoes to overpower the landlord and rob his grain bin.

Nearly always, too, these resources could, in principle, be applied to change the expected behavior of someone else, in a word: to influence others. Frequently, in fact, these resources could be used to create a threat of severe penalties and thus offer the chance of gaining power over others.

Generally, then, human beings have access to some political resources, however paltry these may be. But human beings have many goals. Often, too, they can employ different means to achieve a given goal. Not all men apply their resources to gaining power. Yet some, the power-seekers, do. Why?

The answers to this question can be grouped into three categories.

1. Men seek power, it is said, in order to achieve the collective good. They wish to protect the interests of all citizens, achieve justice for all, benefit the state, or provide for life, liberty, and the pursuit of happiness. This is the argument attributed to Socrates in Plato's *Republic:*

So far as arts are concerned, then, no art ever studies or enjoins the interests of the superior or stronger party, but always that of the weaker over which it has authority.
Thrasymachus assented to this at last, though he tried to put up a fight. I then went on:
So the physician, as such, studies only the patient's interest, not his own . . .; and the ship's captain . . . will study and enjoin the interests of his subordinates, not his own.

He agreed reluctantly.

And so with government of any kind: no ruler, insofar as he is acting as ruler, will study or enjoin what is for his own interest. All that he says and does will be said and done with a view to what is good and proper for the subject for whom he practises his art.[4]

Now the difficulty with this debate between Socrates (or Plato) and Thrasymachus is that the two men are talking right past one another. This often happens in political controversy; each opponent vigorously flails an argument the other did not make, and thereby fails to meet head-on the precise point the other did make. In this case Socrates was making a *normative* argument, Thrasymachus an *empirical* one. Socrates met Thrasymachus' attempt to describe how rulers generally *do* act by indicating how good rulers *ought* to act.

Socrates and Plato knew perfectly well that rulers of states do not in fact always rule in the interests of their subjects. Indeed, to both Socrates and Plato the very meaning of a bad or perverted state was that the rulers did not seek the good of those over whom they ruled. Later on in the *Republic* Plato undertakes a description of the tyrant:

. . . In every one of us, even those who seem most respectable, there exist desires, terrible in their untamed lawlessness, which reveal themselves in dreams. . . . Thus, when nature or habit or both have combined the traits of drunkenness, lust, and lunacy, then you have the perfect specimen of the despotic man. . . . When the number of such criminals and their hangers-on increases and they become aware of their strength, then it is they who, helped by the folly of the common people, create the despot out of that one among their number whose soul is itself under the most tyrannical despotism.[5]

In sum, many political philosophers have argued that leaders *should* seek power in order to exercise authority for the good of all. But probably no student of politics has ever really argued that this is the only reason, or even the principal reason, why men *do* in fact seek power.

2. Men seek power, it has been argued, in conscious pursuit of their self-interest. This was the argument of Thrasymachus that Socrates purported to attack. Thrasymachus had said (according to Plato).

What I say is that "just" or "right" means nothing but what is to the interest of the stronger party. . . . In every case the laws are made by the ruling party in its own interest; a democracy makes democratic laws, a despot autocratic ones, and so on. By making these laws they define as "right" for their subjects whatever is for their own interest, and they call anyone who breaks them a "wrongdoer" and punish him accordingly. This is what I mean: in all states alike "right" has the same meaning, namely what is for the interest of the party established in power, and that is the strongest.[6]

[4] *The Republic of Plato,* translated with introduction and notes by F. M. Cornford (New York: Oxford University Press, 1945), pp. 23–24. The English translations of Plato's *Republic* often vary somewhat, but in the passages quoted here the differences are not significant. The student may wish to compare *The Dialogues of Plato,* translated by B. Jowett (New York: Random House, 1937), Vol. I, pp. 607–608; and *Plato, The Republic,* translated by P. Shorey (New York: Putnam, The Loeb Classical Library, 1930), p. 63.
[5] *The Republic of Plato,* in Cornford, trans., *op. cit.,* pp. 297, 298 and 300.
[6] *Ibid.,* p. 18.

Thrasymachus may well have represented an early Greek attempt to find naturalistic explanations for political behavior. Since nearly all we know of him comes from his enemy Plato, his argument in the *Republic* is probably somewhat distorted. Evidently Thrasymachus was trying to explain how it is that although rulers always proclaim that they are seeking justice, different rulers impose different ideas of justice on their states. To Thrasymachus the obvious explanation of the paradox was that each ruler was simply pursuing his own self-interest; "justice" as it was actually defined in the laws of each state was a mere ideological rationalization for the self-interest of the rulers. It is quite possible that Thrasymachus used his analysis to uphold traditional Athenian democratic institutions against subversion by supporters of oligarchy who insisted that they and they alone were concerned for the good of the state. Undoubtedly he also employed his analysis to undermine the appeal of Plato's elaborate defense of aristocracy, which Thrasymachus probably believed was no more than a brilliant rationalization for the anti-democratic ambitions of the oligarchical faction in Athens.[7]

Thrasymachus' hypothesis that men deliberately seek power for reasons of self-interest has been restated many times. Hobbes, for example, held that men were impelled by their passions and guided by their reason. Passion is the wind that fills the sails, reason the hand on the rudder. Man, to use another metaphor, is a chariot pulled by the wild horses of passion and steered by reason. Men's desires are insatiable, but reason dictates prudence. With the aid of his reason, man can discover the general rules or precepts that will enable him to improve his chances of gaining the ends his passions dictate. All men, then, seek power in order to satisfy their passions. But reason tells them *how* to seek power so as to reduce frustration, defeat, and the chances of violent death.

One difficulty with this hypothesis, as Plato rightly saw, is that the notion of "self-interest," which seems transparently obvious, is actually very complex. What one views as his "self" depends on one's identifications, and evidently these vary a good deal. How one perceives the "self" is not wholly instinctive, it seems, but also a matter of social learning. Likewise, what one considers to be in the "interest" of the self is shaped by learning, experience, tradition and culture. Consequently, to attribute an act to self-interest does not explain very much. As a distinguished modern psychologist has said:

> . . . the self comprises all the precious things and persons who are relevant to an individual's life, so that the term selfish loses its original connotation, and the proposition that man is selfish resolves itself into the circular statement that people are concerned with the things they are concerned with.[8]

Jones' self-interest can mean Jones' pursuit of advantages for himself alone. Or it can mean his attempt to obtain advantages of all kinds for himself and his family. The Jones family now becomes the "self" and its "interests" run from acquisitiveness to zoology. Or Jones' self-interest can mean his attempt to obtain advantages for larger strata with which he identifies—his neighborhood, region, class, religion, ethnic group, race, nation. Thus both the "self"

---

[7] On this point see Eric A. Havelock, *The Liberal Temper in Greek Politics* (New Haven: Yale University Press, 1957), p. 231 and *passim*.

[8] Gardner Murphy, "Social Motivation" in G. Lindzey (ed.), *Handbook of Social Psychology* (Cambridge, Mass.: Addison-Wesley, 1954), 2 Vols., Vol. 2, p. 625. On the influence of social learning on the self, see also E. H. Erikson, *Childhood and Society* (New York: Norton, 1950).

Political Man

with which Jones identifies and the range of ends he regards as in the "interests" of the self may be extremely narrow or very wide, depending on learning, experience, tradition and culture. Anthropological studies testify to the fact that notions of "self," "interest," and "self-interest" vary widely among human beings.

A second objection to rational self-interest as an explanation is posed by post-Freudian psychology. Thrasymachus, Hobbes, Jeremy Bentham, and Marx all interpreted the search for power as "rational" and conscious pursuit of self-interest. But Freud showed that the "desires, terrible in their untamed lawlessness," of which Socrates spoke did more than drive human beings into conflict with one another (as Hobbes argued); they also drive human beings into conflict with themselves. These inner conflicts, according to Freud, are fierce gales that often blow out the flickering light of reason. Reason, as Freud saw it, cannot always guide the chariot drawn by passion, for these violent steeds turn on one another and in their battle the reins of reason become entangled.

Freud discovered, analyzed, and stated what those keen students of human psychology, the great playwrights and novelists, had always known. But since Freud's day, several social scientists have attempted to develop systematic theories dealing with the search for power.

3. Men seek power, some recent students of politics argue, from unconscious motives. One of the most influential contemporary explanations of power-seeking is Lasswell's. His theory can be summarized as follows. The power-seeker pursues power as a means of compensating for psychological deprivations suffered during childhood. Typical deprivations that engender power-seeking are a lack of respect and affection at an early age. The self, then, suffers damage; the individual acquires a low estimate of the self. (The self usually includes more than the "primary ego," the "I" or "me"; it includes parents, wife, children, friends, countrymen, co-religionists and others.) In childhood, adolescence, or perhaps later, the power-seeker learns to compensate for this low estimate of the worth of his "self" by pursuing power. He comes to believe that by acquiring power he can either make the self better, and hence more loved and respected, or he can change the attitudes of others about his "self." With power he will become important, loved, respected, admired. He hopes, then, to acquire through power relationships the affection and respect he failed to acquire in his family relationships. None of this behavior, of course, need be impelled by conscious, "rational" thought. On the contrary, a great deal of the motivation is likely to be unconscious. The power-seeker does not necessarily have much insight into why he seeks power; he rationalizes his power-seeking in terms acceptable to his conscious values and perhaps the prevailing ideology among those with whom he identifies. In comparison with other people, then, the power-seeker is a person who:

a. Places a high value on gaining power.

b. Demands power (and other values) for the self (the primary ego plus incorporated symbols of other egos).

c. Has relatively high confidence that he can gain power.

d. Acquires at least a minimum proficiency in the skills of power.[9]

[9] Harold Lasswell, *Power and Personality* (New York: Norton, 1948), Ch. 3, "The Political Personality," *passim*.

Lasswell himself has questioned whether his power-seeker is likely to be very effective in *achieving* power, since he is likely to stimulate too much dislike and distrust to acquire much support. Robert Lane also argues that a number of recent findings suggest that a strong desire to gain power over other people is not correlated with political activity, at least in democratic systems. Lane furnishes several explanations for this paradox:

a. "To be successful in politics a person must have sufficient interpersonal skills to relate himself effectively to other men and must not be so consumed with power drives that he loses touch with reality. A person with a raging desire for power . . . will constantly alienate his supporters, thereby making the achievement of power impossible for him."

b. "One of the most common sources of the need for power over others is the deeper need for reassurance about the self. . . . This need for reassurance is, of course, related to lack of self-confidence, feelings of unworthiness, or low esteem. (But) . . . a feeling of personal effectiveness is highly related to participation."

c. "The power-seeker may find his needs sublimated in other ways than political activity, at least as this term is ordinarily defined."[10]

CONCLUSION

Of the three explanations for seeking power that we have explored, none seems entirely satisfactory. However, our discussion does suggest several conclusions:

First, whatever the reasons may be, some people do seek power more intently than others.

Second, scientific knowledge about the personalities and motives of power-seekers is still scanty. Everyone agrees that some people seek power more ardently than others, but authorities disagree over why they do.

Third, it seems evident that men seek power not only for its own sake but because of its instrumental value. Power can be used to gain a great variety of ends. Depending on culture, society, economy, and political system, power (as Lasswell and many others have pointed out) can be used to acquire fame, reverence, security, respect, affection, wealth and many other values. It is not surprising, then, that men should seek power; nor should we necessarily assume that power-seeking is abnormal or pathological. In its instrumental character, power is like money. Some men invest more effort in gaining money than others do; they do not necessarily do so because they value money, as such, more highly than others but because they see money as an instrument to other goals.

Fourth, power-seeking, like other behavior, is no doubt usually a compound of conscious and unconscious motives. Men who seek power may know some of the reasons why they do so; we can hardly expect them to know all the reasons.

Fifth, it seems unlikely that all power-seekers have substantially similar personalities. There are too many different reasons, conscious and unconscious, why one might want power, and too many variations in the costs and benefits of power from one political system to another and from one time to

[10] Lane, *op. cit.*, pp. 126–128.

another. Undoubtedly both Caligula and Abraham Lincoln sought power. Yet it is highly implausible to suppose that Caligula and Lincoln had even approximately the same kind of personality.

The Powerful

Not all power-seekers, we have said, gain power. Indeed, though it is probably uncommon, some men who do not seek to gain and wield power may nevertheless exercise it. Why do some people gain more power than others?

In principle, if one gains more power than another (over X, with respect to Y)[11] then we may look to two possible sources of explanation to account for differences in the amount of power—to differences in the amount of resources used, and to differences in the skill or efficiency with which the resources are applied. Some people use more resources to gain power than others do. Some people use what resources they have more efficiently, more skillfully.

Why do some people use more resources than others do to gain power? Presumably because they expect to "gain more" by doing so. I may "gain more" than you from a given action either because the action is "less costly" to me or because the outcome of the action is "more valuable" to me. If A has more resources than B—if, say, A is wealthier than B—then a given outlay is less costly for A than for B (all other things being equal) because A has to forgo fewer alternatives than B. Or, in the language of the economist, A's opportunity costs are lower.

A man of wealth and a good deal of leisure can devote 60 hours a week to non-paying political activities at considerably lower opportunity cost than the man who has to work long hours to make a living. In short, if A has more resources than B, the opportunity costs of allocating a given amount of those resources to gaining power are less for A than for B. A can make the same outlays as B at less opportunity cost or more outlays at the same opportunity cost. In general, then, some people use more resources to gain power than others do because they have access to more resources. And, all other things being equal, it is reasonable to expect that people with more resources would gain more power. To this extent, then, differences in power and power-seeking are related to differences in objective circumstances.

However, "all other things" are not usually equal. Even if their resources were objectively identical, A might allocate a greater share of his resources in order to gain power if he places a higher value on the results. Why might A place a higher value than B on the results of an outlay of resources to gain power?

Because A might expect different results from B.

Because, though both expect the same results, A and B use different values or different scales to appraise the results.

Because, though they expect the same results, A feels more confident about the outcome than B does.

However, A's application of more resources may not result in more power (measured in any of the ways described in the last chapter) if B has

---

[11] For convenience, the clause in parenthesis will be dropped from time to time, though as we saw in the last chapter it would be formally necessary to give more precise meaning to the sentence.

more skill than A. A deft politician may accomplish more with little than a clumsy politician can accomplish with a great deal. Why then do some people have more skill in politics than others?

This is a difficult question to answer. To try to do so would carry on beyond the limits of this book. In brief, however, there are three possible explanations for a difference in skill between two persons, whatever the skill may be, whether walking a tightrope over the Niagara, playing the part of Mimi in "La Boheme," or serving as majority leader in the United States Senate. These are:

1. Genetic differences.
2. Differences in opportunities to learn.
3. Differences in incentives to learn.

The first two are differences in situations, the third is a difference in motivations.

The question we started out to answer a moment ago, you may remember, was, Why do some people gain more power than others? Let us now summarize our explanation.

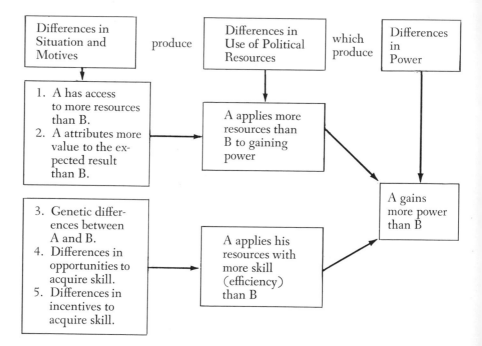

Once again, the argument points to the conclusion that men who gain power need to be similar to one another only in certain formal respects. In fact, the concrete characteristics of leaders seem to vary a good deal in different political systems, different times, and different situations. Leaders have different social origins, different resources, different skills, different personalities. Among those who have sought and gained power, the range of human types runs from Napoleon Bonaparte, the Corsican upstart, to Winston Churchill, descendant of seven Dukes of Marlborough; from Caesar, the

Political Man

military genius, to Woodrow Wilson, historian, political scientist, and college president; from the detached and reflective Hadrian to Savonarola, the fanatic; from the regal Elizabeth the First to Madame de Pompadour, the witty mistress of Louis XV; from the serene stoicism of the philosopher Marcus Aurelius to the neurosis of Hitler and the paranoia of Stalin; from Caligula to Lincoln.

Political Conflict, Coercion, and Popular Government

If everyone were perfectly agreed on ends and means,
no one would ever need to change the way anyone else behaved.
Hence no relations of influence or power
would arise. Hence no political system would exist. Let one person
frustrate another in the pursuit of his goals, and you
already have the germ of a political system. For the one
may then try to change the behavior of the other. If he does so
by creating the expectation of sizeable rewards or deprivations, then
relations of power come into existence.

Conflict and politics are born as inseparable twins. But conflicts can be handled in many different ways, and these different ways do not seem equally attractive to us. Different ways of dealing with conflict are at the heart of every great political alternative debated by political philosophers since the time of the Greeks.

Two Key Questions

If conflict is unavoidable in human society, can coercion of some people by others ever be eliminated in political systems, or if not eliminated, at least minimized? Since few people, if any, regard coercion as intrinsically desirable, this question is bound to be important to everyone who gives serious thought to politics.

There is, however, a second question that is primarily important to those of us who believe in the desirability of democratic institutions. How can conflict be kept within bounds in a democracy so that it does not destroy the system? In the United States, for example, most people undoubtedly believe that one Civil War was enough. Hence it is important for us to identify, and, so far as possible, to establish conditions that will reduce the danger of violence, widespread coercion, and the breakdown of a democracy by civil strife.

This second question raises a ticklish problem of definition. What do we mean by "democracy"? Do we mean a perfect or nearly perfect equality of power? As we have seen, a perfectly equal distribution of power seems to be unattainable; certainly it is in a large industrial society. Consequently, we shall settle here for a more modest objective. We shall consider as democracies political systems like those of the United States, Canada, Britain, the Scandinavian countries, Switzerland, New Zealand, Australia and others in which power over state officials is widely, though by no means equally, shared. What conditions enable political systems like these to solve their conflicts more or less peacefully? This question is more manageable, and it is the one we explore in this chapter.

However, because the term "democracy" is used to label both an unattained and perhaps unattainable ideal, and existing political systems, it is hard to avoid confusing these two meanings. Hence it may help to use different terms. In the rest of this chapter, therefore, we shall use as interchangeable the terms "popular government" and "polyarchy" (rule by many) to refer to political systems like those just listed. We shall consider the term "democracy," which will rarely be used in the rest of this chapter, as a label for the unattained ideal.

Our two questions can now be re-phrased as follows:

1. What kinds of conditions tend to reduce the use of coercion in a political system?

2. What conditions favor the peaceful adjustment of conflicts in a polyarchal system?

Alternatives to Coercion

When two individuals conflict with one another in pursuing their goals, they confront three great alternatives: deadlock, coercion, or peaceful adjustment.

Political Conflict, Coercion, and Popular Government

Deadlock exists so long as each continues to block the other and neither changes his behavior. Deadlock means "no deal." Deadlock is likely to occur whenever individuals disagree and the outcome of the deadlock (often the status quo) seems tolerable.

Imagine two apple-pickers who work side by side. The faster of the two is able to earn $100 a week during the apple-harvesting season; the slower only $50. By cooperating, they could pick even faster and thus could earn a total of $200 a week. But how are they to divide up the gain? Their problem is illustrated in Fig. 10. A's possible earnings are represented by the vertical axis, B's by the horizontal axis. The point marked "status quo" represents the existing situation: A earns $100 a week and B $50. The diagonal line represents all possible ways of sharing $200—from $200 for A and nothing for B all the way to nothing for A and $200 for B. However, it is obvious that neither would cooperate with the other if the yield were less than he expected to gain by maintaining the status quo. Consequently, the hatched area inside the small triangle represents the only set of mutually profitable ways of dividing up the pie; running from one limit, in which A gains virtually all the additional earnings (A, $149.99; B, $50.01) to the other, in which B gains practically all the additional earnings (A, $100.01; B, $99.99). Any agreement they can arrive at would presumably not go beyond these two limits.

Suppose they cannot agree on how to distribute the extra earnings? Then deadlock ensues and the status quo remains. This solution will seem unreasonable to many people; yet individuals often are "unreasonable," particularly if they are unaccustomed to negotiation, have markedly different values, or have little opportunity to negotiate with one another.

In this case deadlock seems "unreasonable" because both stand to gain over their present situation if they can only agree. Often, however, every new solution will make at least one of the parties to the conflict worse off than he is at present. From his point of view, then, maintaining the status quo by deadlock is preferable to peaceful adjustment. In this case the danger is that the parties who could gain from a change may then seek a solution by *coercion,* particularly negative coercion.

Every State uses some coercion to secure compliance with the decisions of the government. Coercion has been a common practice in the relations among states; in international politics war or the threat of war has frequently been used as an alternative to stalemate or peaceful adjustment. Civil wars and revolutions also involve coercion; each side resorts to coercion to impose its will on the others. It is easy for people accustomed to relatively stable political systems like those of Britain and the United States to lose sight of the frequency of revolutions, civil wars, and violence in the political history of the human species. Even today, in large parts of the world civil strife, guerrilla war, revolutionary struggles, violence, and suppressing political opponents by physical force are normal and commonplace political practices. It may help Americans to understand the pervasiveness of "internal war" if they remember that their own Civil War lasted five years and was one of the bloodiest exhibitions of fratricide in modern history.

The major alternative to deadlock or coercion is *peaceful adjustment.* In a peaceful adjustment of a conflict, the parties perceive an alternative more profitable than either deadlock or coercion, and adjust their behavior so as to bring about this alternative. The two apple-pickers, for example, might divide

Political Conflict, Coercion, and Popular Government

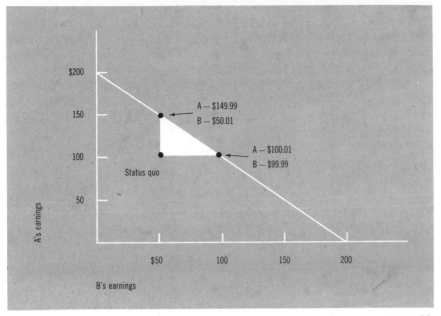

FIGURE 10.

all the mutually beneficial solutions into six possible ways of sharing the additional $50 a week they could earn by pooling their efforts. They could number these solutions from 1 to 6; at the end of each week's work they could throw a die, and whatever number came up would be the solution for distributing that week's extra earnings. Whatever the outcome, then, both men could count on earning more money if they adopted this solution than if they failed to agree on a solution.

Except for pacifists who advocate nonviolence on moral ground, peaceful adjustment is not necessarily the "best" solution in every case. Indeed, few advocates of nonviolence are prepared to extend their program to cover all situations. Even pacifists, for example, would probably not insist that we rely exclusively on peaceful adjustment to solve a controversy between a thief and a lawful owner, to regulate traffic, or to control the sale of drugs.

Before the outbreak of the Civil War, various suggestions for a peaceful adjustment of the dispute were suggested, including proposals that would have given constitutional protection to slavery in the South and barred it in all or some of the rest of the country. Would this peaceful compromise have been preferable to the agony of the Civil War? Although one's answer will reflect many different assumptions about fact and value, many people will hold that slavery was morally more abominable than war and, in this case, peaceful adjustment was not the best course. Because he believed that the Union ought to be preserved intact, Lincoln himself refused to accept the peaceful adjustment that might have been possible if the southern states had been allowed to secede.

However, the costs of physical coercion are often very high. In relations among states in the modern world, the potential cost in human destruction resulting from war have become so enormous that human imagination boggles

Political Conflict, Coercion, and Popular Government

in the attempt to make them palpable. Within states, too, instruments of terror, torture, and death employed by dictators like Stalin and Hitler have demonstrated once again how costly in civilized values the widespread application of coercion can be.

Coercion and Popular Government

It is a profound though not uncommon misunderstanding about popular governments—about "democracies"—to assume that they do not employ coercion. They do. For example, in the United States in 1959 there were 207,513 persons in federal and state prisons. These prisons had over 40,000 full-time employees. Over 300,000 people were employed as policemen by federal, state or local governments. In all American cities over 2,500, out of a total population of 56 million, 2.6 million people were arrested in 1959 for violating the laws; 1 million of these were arrested for drunkenness. From 1930–1960, 3,724 persons were executed by civil authorities in the United States—an average of 124 persons a year.[1] (However, the death penalty was declining; in 1960, with a much larger population than ever before, 57 persons were executed, 45 of them for murder.)

Nonetheless, even though popular governments do employ coercion, they cannot do so effectively unless the violators are few in number and lack support and sympathy among the population at large. In 1959, out of every 100,000 persons in the United States, only 119 were in federal and state prisons.

So long as the institutions of popular government are unimpaired, any attempt to coerce a majority of the population on anything important to them would be certain to fail, for a coerced majority could simply vote against the incumbents at the next election and replace them with more responsive officials. Because of this situation, politicians in polyarchies are rarely so foolhardy as to support laws directed against a majority of the people, except from ignorance of popular opinion.

An attempt to coerce a large number of people, even short of a majority, is unusually difficult in a polyarchy. Extensive coercion places a strain on any political system, even a dictatorship, but popular governments find it most difficult of all. For if civil disobedience on a grand scale, or even civil war, is to be avoided, a government engaged in coercing large minorities needs to have at its disposal an imposing array of coercive forces—a centralized and disciplined police system, a secret police, a compliant judiciary, military and bureaucratic establishments ready to obey the government when "duty" requires the coercion of large numbers of fellow citizens, and a body of law, constitutional doctrine, and practices that permit the government to employ these forces.

So imposing an array of coercion in the hands of the government would be a permanent temptation to unscrupulous leaders and a standing danger to all opposition. Although it is conceivable that a popular government might coerce a large fraction of the population on infrequent occasions, and survive, the more often it did so the more the chances of popular government surviving would be reduced.

[1] *Statistical Abstract of the United States, 1961* (82nd ed., 1961), Section 5, "Law Enforcement, Federal Courts, and Prisons," pp. 137–156.

Political Conflict, Coercion, and Popular Government

If popular governments cannot rely very heavily on coercion, they find deadlock dangerous. Although deadlock is not uncommon in polyarchies, the continued inability of a government to cope with problems that a large body of citizens regards as urgent tends to undermine its legitimacy. For example, the overthrow of the Fourth Republic in France by forces supporting General de Gaulle was precipitated by the frustrations arising out of the long war in Algeria, which the government of the Fourth Republic was not strong enough to end either by a negotiated peace or a military victory.

In general, then, the conditions that decrease the need for coercion and increase the prospects for peaceful adjustment are also favorable to popular government. Let us therefore turn directly to the questions we asked at the beginning of this chapter. Under what conditions can coercion be minimized? Conversely, what conditions favor peaceful adjustment of conflicts? Although answers to these questions are somewhat speculative, there are seven conditions which, it seems entirely reasonable to conclude, favor peaceful adjustment of conflicts.

PURSUIT AND RESOLUTION OF CONFLICTING AIMS

1. *The likelihood of peaceful adjustment to a conflict is increased if there exist institutional arrangements that encourage consultation, negotiation, the exploration of alternatives, and the search for mutually beneficial solutions. Conversely, the propects of deadlock and coercion are increased if institutional arrangements severely inhibit such activities.*

Sometimes institutions are deliberately created to foster peaceful adjustment. In the United States there is a Federal Mediation and Conciliation Service which was established to avert and settle strikes in key industries. The United Nations was intended to provide a forum for the peaceful adjustment of international conflicts.

Long before either of these existed, an institution for encouraging consultation, negotiation, and the exploration of mutually beneficial solutions had already developed. This was the national parliament or legislature. The growth of a legislature, constitutionalism, and later, political parties, has provided modern polyarchies with a special forum where peaceful adjustment of conflicts among different interest groups in a society is strongly encouraged by a complex network of procedures, traditions, rituals, and pressures involving elected representatives, spokesmen for interest groups and experts.

2. *The larger the area of agreement among different actors on what would constitute a desirable solution, the better the chances for a peaceful adjustment.*[2] If everyone were to agree on everything, then no behavioral changes would be required since there would be no conflicts; but political systems exist for the simple reason that perfect harmony does not exist. Even short of perfect harmony, however, a large area of agreement on the properties of "good" solutions to conflicts makes it easier for parties to a conflict to find acceptable solutions. Consider, for example, the classic case of husband and

[2] One should never forget that statements like this carry with them the implicit clause "other things remaining the same." This reservation is equivalent to the familiar process in actual and hypothetical experiments of deliberately changing only one condition at a time and holding all the others constant, in order to see the consequences of a change in the one variable.

wife who disagree on whether they should go to the mountains or the seashore for their vacation. Suppose the other qualities of a good vacation spot they consider are reflected in these alternatives:

a. A natural or rural setting *versus* a resort or urban setting
b. A modest and inexpensive spot *versus* an elegant and expensive place
c. Warm weather *versus* cool weather
d. Strenuous athletic outdoor activity *versus* relaxation

A husband and wife with the same tastes among these four sets of alternatives would find it easier to arrive at an acceptable solution to their conflict over seashore versus mountains than a couple whose tastes conflict on all eight alternatives. Indeed, the more congenial couple might continue their search until they found a perfect solution, say a cottage on a mountain coast. Or they might agree that any solutions satisfactory by any three of the criteria would be acceptable. In short, the greater the zone of agreement on the properties of a good solution, the greater the number of *acceptable* solutions is likely to be.

3. *The more that conflicts are cumulative, the less likely is peaceful adjustment.* This looks very much like the preceding hypothesis, but it stresses the social pattern of conflicts and agreements. In a *cumulative* pattern, if A and B agree with one another and disagree with C and D on one issue, then this same pattern is likely to hold on all other issues. If, for example, A and B support social-security payments to the aged for medical care, and C and D oppose them, then on all other questions on which there is some disagreement among A, B, C, and D, A and B will be on one side and C and D on the other.

A cumulative pattern may be developing or completed. In a developing pattern of cumulative conflict, the disagreements pile up over time. In a community, for example, citizens may first become involved in a hot dispute over the issue of "communism in the public schools"; this issue begins to split the community into two camps; bitterness rises, tempers flare, other issues are dragged in; in time, the town is split right down the middle into two enemy camps that oppose one another not simply on the original issue but on a whole host of other questions as well.[3]

Probably in no political system are conflicts wholly cumulative or wholly non-cumulative, but in a pluralistic pattern conflicts tend to be non-cumulative. People who are in conflict over one issue are not necessarily in opposite camps when the next issue comes up. On some issues, many people are not involved at all; hence different issues may involve different sets of individuals.

James Madison was the prophet of the pluralist pattern, Marx of the cumulative pattern. To meet the fears of many conservatives at the Constitutional Convention of 1787 that conflict would accumulate along lines drawn by regions or class, Madison argued that the dangers of "tyranny" by a majority faction would be solved if the patterns of conflict were pluralistic rather than cumulative. But how could one insure that the pattern in the new Republic here in America would be pluralistic? Simple, Madison replied: The great size and diversity of the United States would be sufficient insurance. In Federalist Paper No. 10, he wrote:

[3] An excellent description of how this process has occurred in a number of different American communities is contained in a short monograph by James S. Coleman, *Community Conflict* (Glencoe, Ill.: The Free Press, 1957).

Political Conflict, Coercion, and Popular Government

Extend the sphere and you take in a greater variety of parties and interests; you make it less probable that a majority of the whole will have a common motive to invade the rights of other citizens.

Like Madison, Marx believed that property was the main source of conflict among human beings. But unlike Madison, Marx held that the pattern of conflict had always been cumulative in the past, was cumulative in his time, and would continue to be cumulative until the progress of socialism established a classless society. Although Marx's description does not seem to apply very well to the United States, in the nineteenth and early twentieth centuries it roughly fitted conditions in Europe. However, extensive social reforms and in recent years a rapidly rising level of individual and collective consumption seem to be creating a pattern of pluralistic conflict in European countries not unlike that in the United States.

4. *The greater the economic "surplus" in a society over and above subsistence needs, the greater the likelihood of peaceful adjustment. Conversely, the greater the "deficit," the greater the likelihood of coercion.* To be sure, "subsistence" is not a precise term. What an Indian villager might regard as quite adequate for subsistence, an American would regard as totally inadequate. Nonetheless, common sense tells us that the average American middle-class family has a much greater "surplus" to dispose of beyond its requirements for subsistence than the family of a villager in India; likewise, the United States in toto has a greater "surplus" to dispose of than India does—which is one reason why we supply foreign aid to the Indians rather than the other way around.

Condition 4 is illustrated in Fig. 11. So long as the amount of goods and services is barely sufficient to cover subsistence needs, as these are defined by the members of the society, then coercion is likely. Any departure from equality of distribution will result in even more severe hardships for some members; hence either equality in distribution will have to be strongly enforced, or else inequalities may have to be protected by state coercion.

How does the existence of a "surplus" facilitate peaceful adjustment? Essentially by increasing the number of conflict situations in which there are mutually profitable solutions. A surplus makes it easier for parties to a conflict to be "bought off."

The United States is a case in point. An American historian, David Potter, has shown how the existence of economic abundance throughout most of our national history has suffused American life and institutions with the spirit of optimism, growth, and mutually beneficial compromise. He has written:

Euuropean radical thought is prone to demand that the man of property be stripped of his carriage and his fine clothes; but American radical thought is likely to insist, instead, that the ordinary man is entitled to mass-produced copies, indistinguishable from the originals. Few Americans feel entirely at ease with the slogan 'Soak the rich,' but the phrase 'Deal me in' springs spontaneously and joyously to American lips. . . . Clearly, if one is leveling a fixed number of items, say, personal incomes, the very process of leveling implies a reduction of the higher ones. But in order to raise the lower without reducing the higher, to level *up*, it is necessary to increase the total of all incomes—that is, to introduce new factors instead of solving the problem with the factors originally given. And it is by this stratagem of refusing to accept the factors given, of draw-

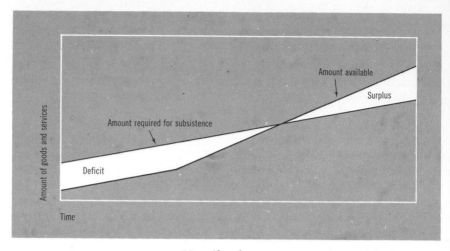

FIGURE 11. *Abundance, poverty, and peaceful adjustment.*

ing on nature's surplus and on technology's tricks, that America has often dealt with her problems of social reform.

Potter then goes on to illustrate how our practice has often been "to over-leap problems—to bypass them—rather than to solve them."

For instance, in the 1880's and 1890's there seemed to be three major public problems—the problem of a shrinking bullion supply; the problem of the control of an entire industry by a small group of monopolists, like John D. Rockefeller and his associates in the oil industry; and the problem of regulation of the railroads, which enjoyed a natural monopoly of transportation. Reformers struggled with all three of these problems, and various political solutions were proposed: the adoption of a bimetallic currency to relieve the bullion stringency, the enactment of an anti-trust law to curb Mr. Rockefeller, and the adoption of an Interstate Commerce Act to protect the shipper vis-à-vis the railroads. But in each case technological change interposed to relieve the acuteness of the problem or even to make it obsolete: the discovery of new gold supplies in the Klondike and of new methods of recovering gold reversed the process of shrinkage in the bullion supply; the discovery of the vast new deposits of oil in Texas and elsewhere undermined the dominance of Rockefeller in the oil industry as no legislative prohibition was ever able to do; and the introduction of trucks moving over a network of national highways ended the natural monopoly of transportation by the railroads before Congress ceased the long quest for a legislative solution.[4]

Conversely, coercion is likely to increase whenever a surplus declines or disappears. A surplus diminishes if the quantity of goods and services available declines (as in an economic depression), if the requirements for "subsistence" increase (as a result of changes in attitudes and ideas current in a society), or if both happen. This helps to explain why many revolutions and other civil disturbances have followed times of rising prosperity, for during long periods in which standards of living are rising, new expectations are created; the grinding poverty of the past is no longer acceptable. Hence when

[4] David Potter, *People of Plenty* (Chicago: University of Chicago Press, 1954), p. 122.

Political Conflict, Coercion, and Popular Government

an economic decline encounters a rising curve of expectations, revolution or other forms of coercion are likely to increase. This seems to have been the sequence of events before Dorr's Rebellion in Rhode Island in 1842, the Russian Revolution of 1917, the Egyptian Revolution of 1952, and a number of other disturbances.[5]

Economic abundance not only facilitates peaceful adjustment in any political system but also creates conditions favorable for the stability of popular governments. Tocqueville wrote in 1835:

> General prosperity is favorable to the stability of all governments but more particularly of a democratic one, which depends upon the will of the majority, and especially to that portion of the community which is most exposed to want. When the people rule, they must be rendered happy or they will overturn the state; and misery stimulates them to those excesses to which ambition rouses kings.[6]

"General prosperity" helps popular government not only by reducing misery and social conflict to manageable proportions but also by making possible a great variety of secondary results. For example, an economic surplus makes it easier for a society to bear the costly burden of universal, free, compulsory education. Indirectly, then, economic abundance is necessary for an educated citizenry. An economic surplus also makes it possible for citizens to enjoy the leisure required if they are to participate in public affairs. (This is why slavery was indispensable to Athenian "democracy." By releasing Athenian males from the arduous struggle for subsistence, slavery thereby enabled free men to become educated and engage in the political life of the city.)

Recent research has helped to confirm the hypothesis that there is a strong relationship between popular government and abundance. For example, S. M. Lipset, a sociologist, has classified European, English-speaking, and Latin-American nations into four groups: (1) European and English-speaking stable democracies (13 countries); (2) European and English-speaking unstable democracies and dictatorships (17 countries, including France, Germany, Italy, Spain and the USSR); (3) Latin-American democracies and unstable dictatorships (7 countries); and (4) Latin-American stable dictatorships (13 countries). Using a number of different indices of wealth, he finds a marked relationship. Among Europeans and English-speaking peoples, the 13 stable democracies are wealthier than the unstable democracies and dictatorships; in Latin America, where there are no truly stable democracies, the indices of wealth are considerably higher among the 7 democracies and unstable dictatorships than among the 13 stable dictatorships. (Fig. 12.)

As one might expect in these circumstances, education follows a similar pattern. In none of the European and English-speaking democracies are more than 5 per cent of the adults illiterate; in the Latin American dictatorships the rate of illiteracy ranges from 24 per cent to 89 per cent.[7] A variety of

[5] James C. Davies, "Toward a Theory of Revolution," *American Sociological Review*, Vol. 27, No. 1 (February, 1962), pp. 5–19.

[6] Tocqueville, *op. cit.*, Vol. 1, p. 300. See also Potter, *op. cit.*, pp. 114–115.

[7] Seymour M. Lipset, *Political Man* (New York: Doubleday, 1960), Chapter 2 "Economic Development and Democracy," pp. 45–72.

Political Conflict, Coercion, and Popular Government

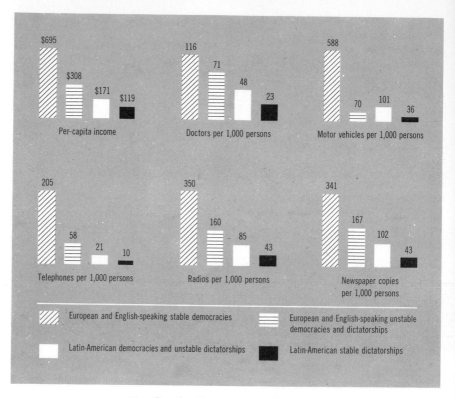

FIGURE 12. *Popular Government and Economic Abundance.* (Source: Adapted from data in Seymour M. Lipset, *Political Man* (New York: Doubleday, 1960), Table II, pp. 51–52. Originally drawn from United Nations Statistical Papers, Series E, No. 1, *Preliminary Report on the World Situation, 1952*; and *United Nations Statistical Yearbook, 1956.*)

indices of education also shows a strong relationship with popular government. (Fig. 13.)

Lack of economic abundance is a powerful factor limiting the spread of popular government in the present world. A large part of the world's population remains even today at the level of bare subsistence. Out of some 66 countries or colonies in Latin America, Africa, and Asia, only three (Venezuela, Uruguay and Israel) had a per capita gross national product above $500 in 1960; indeed in most of these countries the gross national product amounts to less than $200 a person.

Nonetheless it is highly significant that even among the many countries that are economically underdeveloped, the extent to which they approach the institutions and practices of popular government is roughly correlated with their wealth. James S. Coleman classified the political institutions of these 66 nations into "competitive" systems, which possess such basic institutions of popular government as competitive parties, election, and legislatures; "semi-competitive"; and "authoritarian." He then ranked the various countries according to 11 different economic indices. In Latin America, all but 2 of the "competitive" and "semi-competitive" countries are among the 10 wealthiest; all but two of the "authoritarian" countries are among the 10

Political Conflict, Coercion, and Popular Government

poorest. In Asia and Africa the relation, though somewhat less sharp, is nonetheless rather pronounced.[8]

5. *The extent to which peaceful adjustment or coercion is used depends on past experience. The more satisfied people are with the results of past trials, the more likely they are to repeat the same methods. Conversely, the more dissatisfied they are with the results of past trials, the less likely they are to repeat the same methods.* In the period from the writing of the

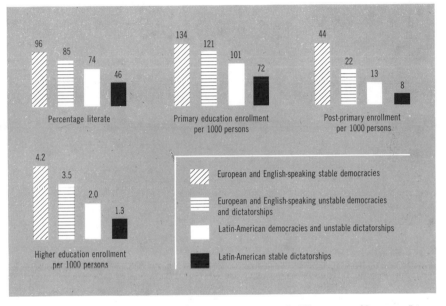

FIGURE 13. *Popular Government and Education.* (Source: Lipset, *op. cit.*)

Constitution until the decade preceding the Civil War, Americans dealt with many problems by peaceful adjustment. The arts of compromise were highly developed; many of the political leaders of the time, like Henry Clay, "the Great Compromiser," were famous for their skills in negotiation and adjustment. From about 1850 onward, however, conditions became less and less favorable for peaceful adjustment of the dispute over slavery. In particular, it became more and more difficult to discover a viable compromise on the question of whether slavery was to be permitted in the western territories; for from the territories, states were to be carved out that might ultimately shift the delicate balance of power between slave states and free states.

Nonetheless, negotiation, adjustment, and compromise were so thoroughly a part of the ethos and practice of American politics that attempts at peaceful adjustment—such as the Crittenden Compromise—went on virtually until the firing on Fort Sumter. The Civil War that followed came to be widely regarded as a deeply tragic national experience. Evidently the grim

[8] James S. Coleman, "The Political Systems of the Developing Areas," in Gabriel A. Almond and James S. Coleman (eds.), *The Politics of the Developing Areas* (Princeton: Princeton University Press, 1960), Tables 3 and 4, pp. 541–542.

Political Conflict, Coercion, and Popular Government

experience of the Civil War strengthened the incentive to avoid a repetition of costly, fratricidal strife. Political energies were directed toward compromise and adjustment, even at the expense of the recently liberated Negro. Most people were weary of war, reluctant to face a new conflict, anxious to get on with immediate tasks. Although Thaddeus Stevens and other Radical Republicans demanded that Congress and the President take firm steps to protect the civil and political rights of the Negroes, they were unable to win sufficient support to carry out their program in full.

Then, following the presidential election of 1876, when the election returns from four states were disputed, a new crisis developed. Neither Hayes, the Republican candidate, nor Tilden, the Democratic candidate, had a majority of uncontested electoral votes. After protracted negotiations that lasted almost until the very eve of the day when a new president was to be sworn in, the decision of an Electoral Commission appointed by Congress was accepted by both sides. The famous (in the eyes of some, infamous) Compromise of 1877 resulted: the Southern Democrats in Congress accepted the Electoral Commission's verdict that all the contested electoral votes should go to the Republican candidate. In return, the Republicans agreed to withdraw Federal troops from the South (thus in effect announcing the end of Reconstruction and the restoration of white supremacy) and to assist the South economically in various ways.[9]

Since 1877 peaceful adjustment has been generally accepted as the normal and preferred method for solving conflicts in the American political system. This does not mean that coercion is always avoided, but it does mean that the use of coercion is markedly less common than it undoubtedly would be if we had not had a century and a half of experience with the relative costs and gains of coercion and peaceful adjustment.

6. *The closer the parties to a conflict approach equality in potential coercive power (as they perceive their situation), the greater the likelihood of peaceful adjustment.* If two parties to a dispute have equal chances of coercing the other, victory becomes both more uncertain and more costly. Conversely, the more unequal are the parties to a conflict, the less costly and the more certain is a coercive victory for the stronger; hence the incentive for the stronger to find a mutually profitable solution is reduced.

The notion of a balance of power in international relations, which since the Renaissance and Reformation "has been a favorite topic of speculation among the political philosophers of Europe,"[10] implies the validity of the sixth condition. The idea itself is exceeding simple:

If all states were held in check, no state could win a war; and, if no state could win a war, then no state would start a war or threaten war. Equilibrium is balanced power, and balanced power is neutralized power. A society in political equilibrium is a society in which force is useless. . . .[11]

[9] For further details on these developments, the student should consult C. Vann Woodward, *Reunion and Reaction, the Compromise of 1877 and the End of Reconstruction* (Boston: Little, Brown, 1951); Paul H. Buck, *The Road to Reunion, 1865–1900* (Boston: Little, Brown, 1938); Roy F. Nichols, *The Disruption of American Democracy* (New York: Macmillan, 1948); Roy F. Nichols, *The Stakes of Power, 1845–1877* (New York: Hill and Wang, 1961).

[10] Nicholas J. Spykman, *American Strategy in World Politics* (New York: Harcourt, Brace, 1942), p. 20.

[11] *Ibid.*, p. 21.

Despite a great deal of talk about balance of power, however, statesmen have rarely sought a nice balance of power, for each prefers that his own country or coalition be slightly stronger than the others. Nonetheless, peace is often maintained simply because no state feels that it has sufficient power to coerce others without suffering equally severe consequences.

When states are convinced that their strength is inadequate to enforce their will, they become peaceful and reasonable, they discover the benefits of conciliation and arbitration and plead in terms of law and justice instead of demanding in terms of force.[12]

To be sure, equality in potential coercive power may lead to stalemate rather than peaceful adjustment. Thus in the 1950's the Soviet Union and the United States did not permit their conflicts over Berlin, East Germany, nuclear testing, and disarmament to develop into war, presumably because both sides feared destruction by the other. The result was stalemate rather than peaceful adjustment, however, since they could not arrive at solutions which both sides regarded as an improvement over the status quo.

The sixth condition also has important implications for popular government. Great inequalities in the distribution of political resources are likely to produce great inequalities in potential coercive power. Hence it has generally been assumed that a stable popular government would be unlikely if political resources were distributed in grossly unequal fashion. "Allow neither rich men nor beggars," Rousseau wrote in *The Social Contract*. "These two estates, which are naturally inseparable, are equally fatal to the common good; from the one come the friends of tyranny, and from the other tyrants. It is always between them that public liberty is put up to auction; the one buys, and the other sells."

However, as we have already seen, the consequences of an unequal distribution of political resources depend a great deal on whether the pattern is one of cumulative or non-cumulative inequalities (Chapter 3, p. 14).

Agricultural societies are particularly prone to cumulative inequalities, for the value of the land a man owns not only determines his total wealth and income but pretty much fixes his social status, educational opportunities, and his political, administrative, and military skills. Hence in an agricultural society, if the distribution of landed property is highly unequal, the distribution of all political resources and skills tends to be highly unequal; consequently, the distribution of power also tends to be highly unequal. This is why a popular government is unlikely to exist in an agricultural society unless landed property is widely distributed with a considerable measure of equality. This point was first stressed explicitly by James Harrington, a seventeenth-century English writer, whose ideas were accepted by many of the men at the American Constitutional Convention. Harrington wrote in *Oceana* (1656):

. . . Such as is the proportion or balance of dominion or property in land such is the nature of the empire.

If one man be sole landlord of a territory, or overbalance the people, for example, three parts in four, he is Grand Seignior; . . . and his empire is absolute monarchy.

If the few or a nobility, or nobility with a clergy, be landlords, or overbalance the people to the like proportion . . . the empire is mixed monarchy . . .

And if the whole people be landlords, or hold the lands so divided among

12 *Ibid.*, p. 25.

Political Conflict, Coercion, and Popular Government

them that no one man, or number of men, within the compass of the few or aristocracy, overbalance them, the empire . . . is a commonwealth.

In short, according to Harrington the distribution of power parallels the distribution of property (in land). One can witness this phenomenon today in many areas of the world that are predominantly agricultural. Thus in Latin America:

. . . land plays a disproportionately large role in the region's economy. It is generally regarded as the chief source of wealth, and land ownership is a mark of prestige. . . .
. . . The class system is a rough measure of the distribution of power in Latin America. The 'whites' and creoles—constituting from 15 to 30 percent of the population of many of the countries—are a species of ruling class. They are the landowners, the political leaders and government officials, the clergymen, almost all of the voters and army officers, and about 90 percent of the people counted as literate.[13]

After the Second World War, one of the first reforms introduced into Japan by the American occupation authorities under General Douglas Mac-Arthur was the redistribution of landed property. The objective was political, not economic; it was taken for granted that popular government was endangered in Japan by the highly unequal distribution of landed property that had prevailed in the past.

Could the United States have developed and maintained institutions of popular government during the period when it was predominantly an agricultural nation without her vast open frontier, which enabled nearly everyone who wished to do so to acquire land? Probably not. "The chief circumstance which has favored the establishment and maintenance of a democratic republic in the United States," Alexis de Tocqueville wrote in 1835, "is the nature of the territory that the Americans inhabit. Their ancestors gave them the love of equality and of freedom; but God himself gave them the means of remaining equal and free, by placing them upon a boundless continent."[14]

If inequalities in an agricultural society tend to be cumulative, what about modern urban industrial societies? Marx held that industrial capitalism must necessarily produce enormous cumulative inequalities. Like Harrington, Marx believed that the distribution of property determined the distribution of all political resources and thereby determined the distribution of power. Since the number of property owners in a capitalist-industrialist society was small relative to the number of propertyless workers, all political resources and hence all power tended to accumulate in the hands of the property owners. Sooner or later, the only resources left to the proletariat would be their numbers and their solidarity—which, however, would be enough to enable them to seize control of the state from the propertied bourgeoisie. By abolishing private ownership of property, socialism would then eliminate the chief source of political inequality.

However, as industrial-urban societies have matured, the distribution of political resources has generally become less extreme. Industrialization

[13] George I. Blankston, "The Politics of Latin America," in Almond and Coleman (eds.), *op. cit.*, pp. 459–462.
[14] Tocqueville, *op. cit.*, Vol. 1, p. 301.

Political Conflict, Coercion, and Popular Government

creates a surplus above bare subsistence; it both requires and makes possible widespread literacy, education, and the growth of a large middle group of professionals and white-collar workers.

Moreover, even though inequalities in political resources persist, cumulative inequality tends to be displaced in mature industrialized societies by a pattern of non-cumulative or dispersed inequalities. Property ownership is only one source of large incomes—artists, entertainers, athletes, professionals, and executives, for example, often earn large incomes. Then, too, "money" is only one kind of political resource. For example, mass communications and urban life make it easier to convert popularity into political influence. New routes are opened up to social standing and prestige. Knowledge, too, is a resource of great significance in highly industrialized societies. Industrial and government bureaucracies require a vast supply of highly educated professionals whose specialized knowledge frequently enables them to exert great influence on decisions.

Thus there appear to be two rather different ways of reducing cumulative inequalities and increasing the chances of popular government. One way is by *decreasing* the degree of inequality in the distribution of political resources—for example, through land redistribution, tax reforms, and expansion of educational opportunities. Harrington in England, Jefferson in the United States, and General MacArthur in Japan all espoused this method for predominantly agricultural societies. The other way is by *dispersing* the inequalities that remain, so that individuals or groups badly off with respect to some kinds of resources are better off with respect to other kinds of resources. This seems to be the pattern that exists in the United States and probably in a number of other mature industrialized nations. The two solutions are not, of course, mutually exclusive; a high stage of industrialization may tend to strengthen both patterns not only by decreasing the extreme inequalities that are mainly a legacy of early industrial systems superimposed on feudalism but also by dispersing the remaining advantages or handicaps to different groups.

7. *Individuals vary in their psychological dispositions toward peaceful adjustment, deadlock, and coercion. Hence the likelihood of peaceful adjustment depends on the personality characteristics of the individuals who influence the decisions of the various parties to a conflict.* The married couple trying to decide where they should take their vacation (in the example cited earlier) might find it impossible to arrive at a mutually agreeable solution if both of them are high-strung, hostile people who fly off the handle whenever they cannot have their way. Immaturity lowers the chances for peaceful adjustment of a conflict; when small children are unsupervised, their games frequently end up in tears and mayhem. Adults too, often have "immature" personalities. Neuroses and psychoses may also impair peaceful adjustment; for example, a person obsessed with paranoid delusions that the whole world is conspiring to destroy him finds it hard to make concessions. Indeed, some people seem to *seek* conflict, in order to punish themselves or to have an excuse for acting aggressively toward others, or perhaps for other reasons.

A psychologist who lived with 70 "aggressive, anti-social, anti-adult boys" at the University of Michigan Fresh Air Camp has drawn an analogy between international aggression and conflicts in that camp. The boys were "recruited from detention homes, training schools, mental hospitals, and

87

clinics throughout the State of Michigan. The camp specializes in children who hate."

Each boy has organized his perception of the world and his position in it along the dimension of toughness, fierceness, fearlessness, and resistance to the influence of others. . . . At once, the boys begin a pattern of militant probing of one another in their individual and group relations seeking to establish a basis for dominance and submission.[15]

The behavior of the boys displays many of the familiar characteristics of international aggression: threats, saber-rattling, recounting past glories, displaying one's allies, deterrence by attack, and the like. The author writes:

Aggressively delinquent boys rarely attack their victims without first provoking them to some hostile act. . . . Among boys who hunger for power, the flimsiest of excuses is deemed sufficient and they are constantly on the alert for the proper opportunity. The most vicious illustration was the case of a boy who hit a 'friend' in the mouth while the 'friend' was taking a mid-afternoon nap. The inhumanity of this act was so threatening to the other boys that the aggressor became the undisputed leader of the group.[16]

Two polar types in political systems are the *agitator* and the *negotiator*.[17] When an agitator is involved in a conflict, the chances of deadlock or coercion are high; when negotiators are involved on all sides, on the other hand, the chances of peaceful adjustment are increased.

A classic modern description of the political agitator is presented by Lasswell:

The essential mark of the agitator is the high value which he places on the emotional response of the public. Whether he attacks or defends social institutions is a secondary matter . . . The agitator easily infers that he who disagrees with him is in communion with the devil, and that opponents show bad faith or timidity. Agitators are notoriously contentious and undisciplined; many reforming ships are manned by mutineers. The agitator is willing to subordinate personal considerations to the superior claims of principle. Children may suffer while father and mother battle for "the cause." . . . The agitator sees "unworthy" motives where others see the just claims of friendship . . . trusts in mass appeals and general principles . . . live(s) to shout and write. . . . They conjure away obstacles with the ritualistic repetition of principles. They become frustrated and confused in the tangled mass of technical detail upon which successful administration depends. . . . They glorify men of outspoken zeal, men who harry the dragons and stir the public conscience by exhortation, reiteration, and vituperation.[18]

Lasswell describes Mr. A., a typical agitator whom he had studied in great detail:

A leading characteristic as moralist, socialist, and pacifist has been his truculence in public. Mr. A. speaks rapidly, with great fervor and earnestness, and his discourse is studded with abusive epithets, sarcastic jibes, and cutting insinuations.

[15] Elton V. McNeil, "Personal Hostility and International Aggression," *The Journal of Conflict Resolution*, Vol. V., No. 3 (September, 1961), pp. 279–290.
[16] *Ibid*
[17] James Q. Wilson describes two similar types, the "militant" and the "moderate" in his study of Negro politics in Chicago: *Negro Politics, The Search for Leadership* (Glencoe, Ill.: The Free Press, 1960), pp. 220–240.
[18] Harold Lasswell, *Psychopathology and Politics* (Chicago: University of Chicago Press, 1930), pp. 78–79.

Political Conflict, Coercion, and Popular Government

He confesses that he has taken an unmistakable pleasure in "rubbing the fur the wrong way." He enjoyed nothing better than accepting an invitation to lecture on social and economic subjects before conservative audiences, and scandalizing them. . . .[19]

By contrast, the negotiator is a compromiser. The agitator feels contempt for the "unprincipled" conduct of the negotiator, whereas the negotiator is baffled by the intransigence of the agitator, who sacrifices immediate gains for abstract principles. The negotiator is more concerned with an acceptable solution to a conflict than a just or perfect solution.

Hence the chances of peaceful adjustment within a political system would appear to be increased, in the short run, if the processes through which leaders are selected tend to recruit negotiators rather than agitators. Thus the Federal Mediation and Conciliation Service consists of experienced labor mediators recruited for their talents as negotiators. When they are invited to mediate a conflict between labor and management, their sole task is to find an alternative acceptable to both sides—and in this way to avoid the deadlock of a strike or coercion by hunger, violence, or government action.

For many social conflicts no conciliation service exists. Yet in popular governments there exists a highly important kind of negotiator who is roughly equivalent to the labor mediator. He is the much-maligned elected politician, the man who spends most of his time trying to win election to office. In order to win elections, the politician has to gain the support of voters, frequently of a majority of voters. To gain the support of voters, the politician has to find ways of conceding to one group as much as possible of what it wants without alienating other groups. This process of coalition-building, which is one of the principal tasks of the elected politician, is the politician's contribution to peaceful adjustment.

But short-run peaceful adjustments may sometimes store up trouble for the future. Paradoxically, then, in a polyarchal system peaceful adjustment may work best in the long run if there are agitators who attack current short-run solutions as unsatisfactory. This view might appropriately be called the Phillips hypothesis, for it was Wendell Phillips, himself a famous American agitator of the nineteenth century, who said that "republics exist only on the tenure of being constantly agitated. The republic which sinks to sleep, trusting to constitutions and machinery, to politicians and statesmen, for the safety of its liberties, never will have any."[20]

The pragmatic politician and the agitator both may contribute to the stability of popular government because—in the extreme case—they hold diametrically opposed views on the importance of current public opinion. The pragmatic politician wants to know what public opinion is; he does not much care what it ought to be. The agitator is interested in what public opinion is only so that he can change it to what it ought to be. The pragmatic politician seeks only to respond to public opinion; the agitator tries to make public opinion respond to him. Wendell Phillips himself made an eloquent if somewhat biased contrast between the agitator and the pragmatic politician:

The reformer is careless of numbers, disregards popularity, and deals only with ideas, conscience, and common sense. He feels, with Copernicus, that as God waited long for an interpreter, so he can wait for his followers. He neither ex-

[19] *Ibid.*, p. 80.
[20] Richard Hofstadter, *The American Political Tradition* (New York: Vintage Books, 1954), p. 138.

Political Conflict, Coercion, and Popular Government

pects nor is overanxious for immediate success. The politician dwells in an ever-lasting NOW. His Motto is 'Success'—his aim, votes. His object is not absolute right, but, like Solon's laws, as much right as the people will sanction. His office is not to instruct public opinion, but to represent it. Thus, in England, Cobden, the reformer, created sentiment, and Peel, the politician, stereotyped it into statutes.[21]

Because he takes current opinion as given, the politician is the instrument of current majorities. Because he takes public opinion as an object to be altered, the agitator helps create future majorities. Both run the fatal risk of being born out of their time. The pragmatic politician born out of his time is obedient to opinions today that lead inexorably to disaster tomorrow. Born out of *his* time, the agitator is merely ignored today and, worse yet, forgotten tomorrow.

Wendell Phillips is the prototype of the intelligent agitator, Abraham Lincoln of the principled politician. Phillips was "an agitator by profession" who "made of agitation an art and a science." He became an abolitionist in the 1830's; after the Civil War he attacked the conciliatory policies of Johnson, supported Radical Republicans like Charles Sumner in Congress, demanded the redistribution of landed property in the South, and thus sought to reduce the power of the ex-slaveholders. He sympathized with the First Socialist International, was "a homespun Yankee" socialist, and supported women's rights. It is understandable that a Virginia newspaper once described him as "an infernal machine set to music."[22]

Although Phillips supported Lincoln during the Civil War, the two could hardly have been more different. Lincoln was surely one of the greatest of our pragmatic politicians. If it is hard to imagine Phillips as President, it is difficult to think of Lincoln other than as President. Yet before he entered the White House he had spent most of his mature life acquiring and practicing the arts of the pragmatic politician. At an early age, in Richard Hofstadter's words, he learned "the deliberate and responsible opportunism that was later so characteristic of his statecraft."

The clue to much that is vital in Lincoln's thought and character lies in the fact that he was thoroughly and completely the politician, by preference and by training. It is difficult to think of any man of comparable stature whose life was so fully absorbed into his political being. Lincoln plunged into politics almost at the beginning of his adult life and was never occupied in any other career except for a brief period when an unfavorable turn in the political situation forced him back to his law practice. His life was one of caucuses and conventions, party circulars and speeches, requests, recommendations, stratagems, schemes, and ambitions. 'It was in the world of politics that he lived,' wrote Herndon after his death. 'Politics were his life, newspapers his food, and his great ambition his motive power.'[23]

In addition to the agitator and the negotiator, another interesting pair of polar types are the "democratic" man and the "despotic" man. Is it possible to specify a kind of personality or character that is especially suited—or unsuited—to the operation of popular government? Plato thought so; in the Republic he vividly sets out his description of "the oligarchic, democratic,

[21] *Ibid.*, pp. 138–139.
[22] For these and other details of Phillips' life see "Wendell Phillips: The Patrician as Agitator," Chapter VI, in Hofstadter, *supra*.
[23] Hofstadter, *op. cit.*, pp. 95–97.

Political Conflict, Coercion, and Popular Government

and despotic characters" and offers explanations as to how these come about.[24] In one form or another, Plato's general hypothesis has been affirmed many times—among others, by Machiavelli.[25]

However, empirical information bearing on Plato's hypothesis is still lacking despite a good deal of speculation that, at least in recent years, has been aided by the insights of modern psychiatry and psychoanalysis. Is there a "democratic" personality? After examining the recent literature on the subject, a recent writer remarks that "Almost all the modern students of national character are convinced that the answer to this question is in the affirmative. Systematic empirical evidence for this faith is unfortunately lacking."[26] Nonetheless, among recent students of politics who deal with this question there is "an extraordinary degree of agreement about the values, attitudes, opinions, and traits of character" that help to maintain a popular system. The most important are attitudes toward one's self, toward others, toward authority, toward the community, and toward values:

1. *Toward self.* A belief in the worth and dignity of one's self.
2. *Toward others.* A belief in the worth and dignity of others.
3. *Toward authority.* A stress on personal autonomy and a certain distance or even distrust of powerful authority; in contrast to the authoritarian, the absence of a need to dominate or submit.
4. *Toward the community.* Openness, ready acceptance of differences, willingness to compromise and change.
5. *Toward values.* A pursuit of many values rather than a single all-consuming goal, and a disposition to share rather than to hoard or monopolize.[27]

Is there an anti-democratic or despotic personality? Since 1950 a good deal of important exploratory work has been carried out on the characteristics of a syndrome termed the "authoritarian personality." A person with an authoritarian personality is said to have the following characteristics:

1. *Conventionalism.* Rigid adherence to conventional, middle-class values.
2. *Authoritarian submission.* Submissive, uncritical attitudes toward idealized moral authorities of the ingroup.
3. *Authoritarian aggression.* Tendency to be on the lookout for, and to condemn, reject, and punish people who violate conventional values.
4. *"Anti-intraception."* Opposition to the subjective, the imaginative, the tender-minded.
5. *Superstition and stereotype.* The belief in mystical determinants of the individual's fate; the disposition to think in rigid categories.

[24] This discussion will be found in Cornford's translation, *op. cit.,* from p. 268 ff. For the democratic character, see pp. 280 ff.

[25] E.g., in his *Discourses on the First Ten Books of Titus Livius,* First Book, Chs. 16, 17 and 18, in Niccolo Machiavelli, *The Prince and the Discourses* (New York: Random House, 1940), pp. 160–168.

[26] Alex Inkeles, "National Character and Modern Political Systems," in Francis W. K. Hsu, *Psychology and Anthropology, Approaches to Culture and Personality* (Homewood, Ill.: The Dorsey Press, 1961), pp. 172–208.

[27] This list is adapted in slightly modified form from a list of Inkeles, *ibid.* Inkeles in turn draws heavily on Lasswell, whose work on democratic character is the modern seminal source. Cf. particularly Lasswell's *Democratic Character* in *The Political Writings of Harold D. Lasswell* (Glencoe, Ill.: The Free Press, 1951), pp. 465–525. See also Karl Mannheim, *Freedom, Power, and Democratic Planning* (New York: Oxford University Press, 1950), Chapter 9, "The Pattern of Democratic Personality," pp. 228–245.

6. *Power and "toughness."* Preoccupation with the dominance-submission, strong-weak, leader-follower dimensions; identification with power figures; exaggerated assertion of strength and toughness.

7. *Destructiveness and cynicism.* Generalized hostility, vilification of the human.

8. *"Projectivity."* The disposition to believe that wild and dangerous things go on in the world; the projection outward of unconscious emotional impulses.

9. *Sex.* Exaggerated concern with sexual "goings-on."[28]

A scale—originally called the Fascism scale and now widely known as the F-scale—was developed from a series of questions designed to tap these underlying attitudes. Individuals with a high degree of "authoritarianism" as measured by this scale are, in comparison with individuals low in "authoritarianism," more likely to display religious, ethnic and racial prejudices, to be ethnocentric, to be intolerant of views with which they disagree, to be dogmatic, and to approve of strong, domineering leaders.

Do individuals with "authoritarian personalities" actually *behave* in politics in ways different from other people? Specifically, are they more anti-democratic in their *overt* actions? Do they, for example, actually join and support anti-democratic political movements? Unfortunately, the answers to these questions are somewhat uncertain. The connection between personality and overt political actions is complex, obscure, and apparently rather loose. In a predominantly "democratic" culture, where democratic norms, institutions, and practices have a high degree of legitimacy, some individuals with "authoritarian personalities" may, conceivably, acquire an overlay of democratic beliefs and habits that help them to function "democratically." Nonetheless, it is certainly a reasonable hypothesis that in a population composed *mainly* of individuals with strongly "authoritarian personalities," a popular government would have great difficulty surviving.

[28] T. W. Adorno, Else Frenkel-Brunswik, Daniel J. Levinson, and R. Nevitt Sanford, *The Authoritarian Personality* (New York: Harper, 1950), p. 228.

Political Conflict, Coercion, and Popular Government

Political
Evaluation

C H A P T E R   E I G H T

One could passively contemplate politics, perhaps,
without making decisions—but it would be extraordinarily difficult
to do so. Even to decide which of two or more alternative
hypotheses is true requires a choice. In any case, one cannot
participate actively in political life without
making decisions. Indeed, is this not what we mean by political action?
Political action, like other human actions, consists
in making decisions—in somehow choosing among alternatives,
and then trying to make one's choices effective.

93

Some of the most important and interesting political decisions are presented by questions like these:

1. What kind of political structure is best?
2. Who is best qualified to rule?
3. What are the best policies for the government to prescribe and enforce?

Answers to these questions can be sought at several different levels of generality. At the most general level, one may try to decide what is, abstractly considered, "the best," assuming the most favorable circumstances possible. At a much more specific level, one may try to decide which is the best alternative available among those in a specific, concrete situation. The most general level of inquiry is the domain of political philosophy; general answers are also contained in many ideologies. Thus to the question, "What kind of political structure is best?" the answer of some philosophers is: democracy. This is the answer prescribed by the prevailing American ideology. But of course different philosophers and different ideologies provide different answers.

The more specific level has sometimes been called the domain of applied politics. This is not a particularly apt title, however, since it suggests that concrete decisions can be made simply by applying the general principles gained at the more abstract level of political philosophy. But the extent to which it is possible or useful to apply abstract notions of "the best" to specific political situations is itself a controversial question, as we shall see. It might be better, therefore, to call this more specific level of inquiry and action the sphere of optimal political decisions. Optimal political decisions may not be the "best" or the "perfect" solutions—they are only the best possible decisions given the constraints imposed by the specific situation. Thus in his *Discourses,* Machiavelli advocated a republic as the best political system; but a republic, he pointed out, requires a virtuous citizenry. In *The Prince,* on the other hand, he seems to be arguing that since the people and leaders of Italy in his day lacked the civic virtues necessary to a republic, the best system possible for Italians, at least for the time being, was a strong leader capable of unifying the entire peninsula. Thus Machiavelli's decision about what was optimal for Italy, given the specific limitations of his day, was not "the best" but rather the "best possible."

Appraisals and Decisions

One's decisions are influenced by the way one appraises the world and one's place in it. Whenever you make a decision about buying a car, taking a job, going on a vacation, voting in an election, or confirming the relative desirability of democracy over dictatorship, you are making appraisals. In a rather abstract sense, the types of appraisals you make are the same whether you decide among alternative political systems at the highly general level of political philosophy or try to make an optimal political decision in a specific situation. The substance and content of appraisals, of course, vary enormously. You are not likely to use the same information to make decisions about automobiles and presidential candidates. The quality of appraisals and the methods for making them also vary enormously. The appraisals on which a decision is based may be conscious or unconscious, simple or complex, deliberate or hasty, based on considerable information or little, wise or stupid.

94

Political Evaluation

What, then, are some of the principal kinds of appraisal that influence decisions?

1. First, one's decisions depend on what one considers to be the *alternative courses of action,* if any, that are "open" or "available." If only a single course of action is open, you have no decision to make. A man falling from an airplane without a parachute cannot decide where he is going to land. Conversely, whenever you are confronted by two or more alternative courses of action, a decision has to be made. In this case even choosing to "do nothing" is a decision. Where there are no elections, citizens do not have to decide whether or how to vote; but if there is an election with two candidates competing for office, you are eligible to vote, and you are aware of the election, then you have at least three alternative courses of action available to you: to vote for one or the other of the candidates, or not to vote at all. You may not be aware, of course, of all the alternatives that exist. Alternatives may be objectively available but, because you are unaware of them, subjectively unavailable. One of the important purposes of political analysis is to increase one's awareness of the range of possible alternatives in politics.

2. Second, one's decision depends on what one believes are *the likely consequences of pursuing each of the alternative courses of action.* Whether you vote in an election contest between A and B, and if you do, whether you vote for A or B, will be influenced by what you think will happen—that is, by your *predictions.* Will things go on much the same no matter what you do? What will A do if he is elected? Or B? Your estimates about the future may be quite limited, and even wholly unconscious, but without *some* predictions concerning what is likely to happen you would have no grounds for choosing any of the alternatives. In this case you might decide to delegate the specific choice—either by letting someone else make the choice for you, or by letting your choice depend on a chance process like tossing a coin.

3. Third, one's decisions depend on the *value* one assigns to the consequences of each alternative. If candidate A is likely to behave in some ways different from candidate B, do the differences matter to you? If they do, which set of consequences are more important to you? To the extent that you draw on your general standards to determine values in the particular case, your decision will be influenced by your general standards of value. However, assigning values is often an extremely difficult process—among other reasons, because your private or even unconscious values may conflict with your public or conscious ones.

These three kinds of appraisals would be the most important ones in situations where you assume that the consequences of each alternative are virtually certain to occur. For example, suppose that you are a member of a legislative body. A bill that on balance you wish to defeat has received a tie vote, and you as presiding officer are entitled to cast a deciding vote. You know, then, that your vote will certainly kill the bill. In this case your decision is relatively simple. But as even this example suggests, one generally cannot be certain of the consequences—not, at any rate, of *all* the consequences. Suppose, for example, that you oppose the bill on principle but are uncertain about the attitudes of your constituents? Or, indeed, suppose you think it highly probable that certain key groups in your constituency will swing over to your opponent in the next election if you oppose this bill, and highly unlikely that you will gain support from other groups by opposing it? The decision now becomes more complex. How important to you is your re-election? How likely are the various and somewhat uncertain consequences?

Because of the obviously critical importance of *uncertainty*, decisions are often influenced by several additional kinds of appraisals.

4. Fourth, then, in situations of uncertainty, one's decision depends on one's guesses, hunches, or estimates concerning the *probability that the various consequences will actually occur*. Many differences over policy can be traced to differences in estimates of the likelihood of different consequences. Two people may agree substantially on the alternatives, the *possible* consequences of each, and on their evaluation of the different sets of consequences, and yet may disagree on policy because their estimates concerning the likelihood of the consequences are different. For example, in early 1942 President Roosevelt ordered the evacuation from the West Coast of all people of Japanese origin, many of whom were American citizens, on the advice of military commanders who said that there was a very high probability of mass uprisings, sabotage, and espionage among the Japanese-Americans on the Pacific Coast. At the time and later, the decision was severely criticized as unnecessary and unjust on the ground that widespread acts of disloyalty among the Japanese-Americans were in fact a very remote possibility. Indeed, the Attorney General of the United States and director of the Federal Bureau of Investigation believed on the basis of their evidence (which, it appears, was never presented to President Roosevelt) that the disloyal elements among the Japanese-Americans were very small in number and could be easily identified. Had President Roosevelt accepted the estimates of the Department of Justice concerning the probability of disloyal action, doubtless he would not have issued the executive order. But instead he accepted the estimates of the military, and the order followed.

5. Fifth, in situations of uncertainty, your decision will depend on your *orientations toward risk, uncertainty, and gambling*. A cautious person who only bets on a sure thing is unlikely to advocate the same policies as a more adventurous person who likes to take risks. (Of course a person who is adventurous in one kind of situation may be cautious in another.) Despite the obvious importance of different orientations toward uncertainty, not much is known about them. Moreover, philosophers who have written about problems of ethics and values have not paid much attention to differences in orientations toward risks and uncertainties. Yet many differences over policies and decisions must turn on different orientations toward uncertainty.

Suppose you are confronted by two alternatives. One seems to offer about an equal chance of brilliant success and dismal failure; if you choose the other, the chances of failure seem to be very small but the gains, though relatively certain, are also very small. Is there a "rational" or "best" choice in cases like this? Is it more rational to invest in stocks and hope for large gains or to invest in bonds and count more confidently on small gains? How far should the United States go in risking nuclear war? It might well be argued that American willingness to risk an all-out war is an indispensable condition for success in negotiating with the Soviet Union or China—that, indeed, peace depends on our being willing to risk a nuclear war. Yet there is some probability that negotiations will fail and mutual annihilation will occur. How much should we be willing to take this chance? Should we follow a cautious policy that reduces the risks of precipitating nuclear war

Political Evaluation

even if it increases the probability that Soviet and Chinese power will expand?

Over the last several decades, mathematicians, logicians, and others have sought to develop criteria of "rational" or "best" decisions for uncertain situations like these, using mathematical models derived from two rather new and related kinds of mathematics, the theory of games and statistical decisions. Unfortunately, however, the more elegant and convincing the mathematical formulations, the more they apply to extremely simple human situations, and, therefore, the less they seem relevant to the complex problems of real life. Conversely, when mathematicians attempt to grapple realistically with highly complex decisions, they find it necessary to introduce more and more assumptions resting on common sense, intuition, or their own personal values. For most crucial decisions, mathematical models have proved so far to be of slight value.[1]

Nonetheless, these recent developments in mathematics have emphasized much more sharply than philosophers had before that it is usually not enough to know which outcome is "the best" in order to make a decision. Frequently one cannot simply apply one's standards of values to the different possible results of a decision, determine which one is "the best," and then choose it. For if there is *uncertainty* about the outcomes, to choose "the best" might be to adopt a strategy that most people on careful reflection would surely reject. For example, let us suppose that one *possible* outcome of foreign policy A is an international system that will insure permanent peace; but a much more *likely* outcome of this policy is thermonuclear war. On the other hand, the most likely outcome of foreign policy B is another decade of stalemate without either war or guaranteed peace. The chance that B will produce an international system of peace and order is virtually zero, yet the chance that it will lead to war is rather low. On reflection most people would, I suspect, prefer B to A, even though one possible result of A might be, in their view, far and away the "best" of all solutions.

All this is just another way of approaching the distinction made earlier between the domain of "the best" and the domain of the optimal, or between the sphere of political philosophy and the sphere of concrete decisions and policies. To move from "the best" to the optimal, we are now beginning to see, can be a very complex business.

We have seen that your decisions, whether about politics or other matters, are influenced by:

1. The alternatives "open" or "available" to you.
2. The likely consequences of each alternative.
3. The value to you of each set of consequences.
4. Your estimate of the relative probability of the consequences.
5. Your attitudes toward risk and uncertainty.

So far we have made no effort to distinguish between good and bad appraisals, or between wise and foolish decisions. Now we are going to con-

[1] This is a somewhat tendentious judgment with which some mathematical model-builders would disagree. But it represents the sober conclusion of most informed students of policy-making, I believe, after two decades of work by games theorists and others to demonstrate the worth and relevance of their wares.

sider some (though by no means all) of the important factors that affect the *quality* of one's appraisals.

As an inspection of the preceding list reveals, from the very outset the quality of your appraisals is bound to be influenced by your conception of just what alternatives are really available to you. Probably every reader can recall some instance where he made what he now considers a bad decision, a decision he now regrets, because he was unaware of an alternative that he later realized was objectively available.

An alternative is objectively *available* to you if there is a very high probability that you can in fact perform the actions specified in the alternative. Making the first solo flight across the Atlantic was an alternative available to Charles E. Lindbergh in 1927; flying to the moon was not. But an alternative is *relevant* to you only if there is some chance, however small, that if you do perform these actions, you will be better off than you would be had you not acted in this way. Ordinarily, then, you are concerned not with all the alternatives that may be available to you but only with the smaller set of alternatives that are available and *relevant* to your values.

The extent to which you are fully aware of alternatives depends both on your knowledge and on your focus of attention. You may know perfectly well which exit from a super-highway will enable you to get most quickly to your destination, and yet miss the exit because of inattention. You may be aware of an alternative but fail to explore it because you are preoccupied with other matters. President Roosevelt's decision to order the evacuation of Japanese-Americans from the West Coast was partly a result of his focus of attention at the time. His decision was made shortly after the United States had entered World War II, and his attention was focused on problems of military strategy and mobilization rather than on problems of justice and civil rights. Perhaps because of this, he did not ask the views of his Attorney General about the merits of evacuating the Japanese-Americans; in fact he never fully explored the alternative of simply leaving the Japanese-Americans where they were.

Two of the most important ways of exploring alternatives are by speculation and by science. Speculation is an important prior stage in the growth of scientific knowledge. Philosophers had speculated about the Universe centuries before Copernicus; indeed, even with Copernicus the theory of a heliocentric solar system rested on highly speculative reasoning. Speculation preceded Columbus' discovery of the new world. In politics some of the most important kinds of speculation are in the form of imaginary political systems, or utopias. Plato's *Republic* is perhaps the most influential utopia ever written, because it has caught the imagination of countless generations of readers and made them aware of the possibilities of a state ruled by the most gifted citizens—and aware, also, of some of the problems in achieving such a system. Many modern writers have explored inverted utopias where evil, unpleasant, or objectionable principles rather than good ones dominate the system; thus Aldous Huxley in *Brave New World* and George Orwell in *1984* portrayed inverted utopias to focus the attention of their readers on the dangerous potentialities each saw in contemporary life. Although utopian thinking may generate alternatives that are irrelevant, the portrayal of an imaginary political system may also enlarge the range of alternatives under consideration.

Profiting by speculation and chance discoveries, science opens up new alternatives and often closes out old ones. Frequently the alternatives suggested by speculation are irrelevant until they have been more fully developed by science. No responsible government would have undertaken a space program simply because Jules Verne's novels opened up the possibility of a manned flight to the moon. But developments in science and engineering have made that alternative seem relevant.

These remarks point to a second factor that helps determine the quality of one's appraisals: *the amount and validity of one's factual information.* Two of the five kinds of appraisal in our list consist of evaluations of factual or empirical knowledge. These are the second (the likely consequences of each alternative) and the fourth (the estimate of the relative probability of these consequences). These two factual or empirical appraisals are in effect *predictions.* Predictions are the domain of empirical science rather than philosophy; growth in empirical sciences—whether in the natural sciences or the social sciences—means growth in the reliability of predictive knowledge.

It is obvious that reliable predictive knowledge about human and social systems has been very much harder to gain than reliable empirical knowledge about physical or strictly biological systems. Hence much of the predictive knowledge used in making political decisions must be, in the absence of anything better, at a relatively low level of reliability. Much political knowledge is pre-scientific or non-scientific in character; often one must draw on prevailing common-sense notions (with full awareness that the common sense of one generation is frequently seen as childish nonsense by a later generation). Often, too, one must rely on inference from a woefully limited and unanalyzed body of experiences. A person who refused to make political decisions unless they were based on empirical knowledge at a high level of scientific validity would be paralyzed. Yet in politics "refusing to decide" is simply deciding to allow others to decide for you. Hence, anyone who makes political decisions must, more often than not, act on very incomplete factual information.

A third factor that helps to determine the quality of one's appraisals is *one's values and one's capacity for applying these values* to the various possible outcomes. In particular, the quality of two of the five kinds of appraisals discussed earlier depend on this capacity. They are (3) the value one assigns to each set of consequences and (5) one's orientation toward risk and uncertainty.

Strictly speaking, no amount of factual knowledge will be sufficient to make the appraisals required for (3) and (5). For these appraisals depend on standards of values. No matter how much empirical knowledge one might have about the effects of the death penalty as compared with life imprisonment—no matter how reliable one's predictions might be—one could not decide which alternative is better without criteria for distinguishing "the best" or "the better" consequences from the others. Likewise, no matter how much empirical knowledge one has about the way in which different political systems operate, one cannot decide whether one is better than another without invoking standards of value.

What about the quality of the standards of value themselves? Are some standards of value better than others for appraising politics? If so, the quality of one's appraisals will obviously depend on the quality of one's standards. If not, does it follow that the quality of one's appraisals depends entirely on one's grasp of the alternatives and one's appraisals of the empirical knowledge? Or can we say that even among people with the same standards of values, some apply their values more intelligently than others to the concrete situation?

These questions touch on a number of particularly knotty and acutely controversial problems. Hence we must now face up directly to some of the most hotly disputed issues in modern political analysis. These are:

1. What are the proper sources, grounds, or foundations for political values?

2. What is the proper relation in political analysis between facts or empirical knowledge and values? This question has two parts.

    (a) Can the study of politics be ethically neutral?

    (b) In any case, *should* it be?

3. How are political ideas related to institutions and interests?

The Grounds of Values

Modern political analysts sharply and even bitterly disagree in their answers to the first question. In this respect political analysis is simply a facet of contemporary intellectual life, where many different and conflicting philosophies of value compete for support.

The analysis of this book is, I believe, consistent with a number of different answers to the first question. Consequently, since it would be absurd to try to give a fair and responsible answer to one of the most difficult and hotly contested issues of modern philosophy in the few pages available here, I shall simply indicate briefly the principal kinds of answers that have been given to our question.

1. Political values must rest ultimately on God's will. His will may be known through a direct revelation to an individual or agent (as with Moses and the Ten Commandments) or indirectly by means of reason, or intuition, or experience. Variants of this view are found among many Christian theologians, philosophers, and political analysts, and particularly among Roman Catholics.

2. Political values must rest ultimately on natural laws. Natural laws may or may not be laid down by God. Some writers like Kant or the contemporary American political philosopher Leo Strauss hold that knowledge of natural law can be acquired through reasoning. The distinguished French Roman Catholic philosopher Jacques Maritain would rely more heavily on intuition as a guide in our search for natural law.

3. Political values, like other values, can be derived solely by the methods of the empirical sciences. Not many writers have held this position. Probably the best known is the late American philosopher John Dewey. Although Dewey's argument is somewhat ambiguous, it appears to run directly counter to a central premise of this chapter—namely, that knowledge of values is significantly different in character from the kind of knowledge found in the empirical sciences. Because of the importance of this question, we shall return to it in a moment.

4. Political values, like other values, rest simply on preferences. This position is often associated with Logical Positivism, a philosophical position developed in Vienna in the 1920's among a circle of philosophers who drew heavily on modern science, logic, and mathematics. Some of the early Logical Positivists went even further and held that since value statements are "merely" expressions of preference, they are "meaningless." Today, however,

Political Evaluation

many Logical Positivists agree that although there is no way of providing an "ultimate" justification of values, this does not mean that statements of values are "meaningless." The view that one's values cannot be attributed to Divine will, natural law, or some other ultimate anchoring outside personal preference is also held by many persons who are not Logical Positivists. It is, in fact, the view of many modern writers who are not at all interested in science and logic but are profoundly concerned with the moral and political predicament of modern man. For example, many Existentialists, such as the French philosopher and writer Jean Paul Sartre, hold this view, as well as others whose philosophical stance is less easily classified, such as the late French writer and moralist Albert Camus.

Those who advocate the first three positions contend that values are "universal." By reasoning, intuition or other processes, men of good will must ultimately agree. The fourth position denies that values are necessarily universal; even men of good will may adopt and defend conflicting values. There is, however, a fifth position that serves as a kind of bridge between the first three and the fourth.

5. Some writers hold that though values rest simply on preferences, certain kinds of preferences are probably universal. Some preferences are probably inherent in being human. Hence it should be possible to discover these universal preferences and to construct political systems consistent with them. This view has recently been sympathetically explored by Arnold Brecht, an American political scientist, who concludes: "Strong prima facie evidence indicates that there are . . . universal and invariant 'inescapable' elements in the human way of thinking and feeling about ethical values, and especially about justice."[2]

Facts and Values: Can Political Analysis Be Neutral?

How neutral or objective can the study of politics be? How neutral or objective ought it to be?

Perhaps no other philosophical questions arouse deeper emotions among students of politics. Much of the writing in response to these questions is polemical in spirit and substance. As often happens in polemical debates, opposing positions are frequently distorted; false accusations easily pass for fact. Beneath all the angry rhetoric, however, there is a much larger area of agreement and a much smaller area of controversy than one might surmise from a quick look at most of the contributions to the debate.

Although the answers to these questions are really quite varied, it is possible to distinguish (very roughly) two opposing positions. One group holds that a substantial and important aspect of politics is purely empirical, and that this empirical aspect of the politics can be analyzed (in principle at least) neutrally and objectively. Since the people who hold this position subscribe in effect to the view that an empirical science of politics is possible, let us call them Empirical Theorists. Their opponents hold that for a variety of reasons nothing of great significance can come from an attempt at a purely

[2] Arnold Brecht, *Political Theory, The Foundations of Twentieth Century Political Thought* (Princeton: Princeton University Press, 1959), p. 401. Although written in support of a particular point of view, which he calls Scientific Value Relativism, Brecht's book is by all odds the most comprehensive and most fair-minded summary of the various alternative approaches to political values sketched out above, as well as many others.

scientific study of politics. The study of politics neither can nor should be purely scientific. Let us call these people the Trans-empirical Theorists.

First, then, *can* the study of politics be objective? If we ignore the purely rhetorical arguments in which advocates put up straw men which they then triumphantly knock down, it appears that the Empirical Theorists and the Trans-empiricists both substantially agree on the following propositions:

1. The values, interests, and curiosity of an investigator influence his choice of topics—what he considers interesting, important, and worthy of investigation. This is as true in the natural sciences as in the social sciences.

2. It is impossible to establish criteria of importance and relevance *entirely* from empirical knowledge. One requires values of some kind to decide whether it is more important to understand the different conditions under which democracies and dictatorships are relatively stable than the legislative procedure in the East Pilchard Rotary Club.

3. To aspire to an objective analysis of politics presupposes that one values truth. One must believe that it is worthwhile to distinguish truth from falsehood.

4. Whether they deal with men or atomic particles, all empirical sciences logically rest on assumptions that cannot themselves be established by the methods of the empirical sciences. For example, all empirical sciences take for granted that the universe is "regular" or "lawful" rather than completely random. The laws of science are an expression of confidence in the assumption that relationships that have always held in the past will not change without cause. A hydrogen atom will have the same weight relative to an oxygen atom tomorrow as it had yesterday. Yet the assumption which every scientist makes that because the Universe seems to have been lawful in the past it will be so in the future is a philosophical assumption.

5. In practice, the biases of an investigator may induce him to misread his observations and evidence. This sometimes happens in the natural sciences, too. But in the natural sciences an investigator does not gain acceptance for an hypothesis or theory simply on his own say-so. His procedures, usually experimental procedures, ordinarily can be duplicated by other members of the scientific community. And until others have verified his conclusions to their own satisfaction, his scientific peers are inclined to suspend judgment. Hence in the natural sciences there is a built-in corrective for bias and distortion—so much so, in fact, that a well-trained scientist generally double-checks his own results before publishing them.

In the social sciences, and perhaps most of all in the study of politics, experimental procedures and other forms of rigorous analysis are often impossible or unsuitable for testing a hypothesis or theory. Indeed the "grander" or more comprehensive the theory, the more difficult it is to test. For example, the biases of the investigator can be controlled more easily in voting surveys, where other observers can duplicate the survey or even re-analyze the original questionnaires or IBM cards, than in, say, ambitious historical theories like those of Marx or Toynbee about the rise and fall of political and social systems.

6. Objectivity, neutrality, the capacity and opportunity for scientific detachment are impossible without certain social and political prerequisites. For a scientist to be free to describe the empirical world as he understands it requires rulers willing to tolerate his freedom of inquiry, or even to support it. Yet rulers have theories, too. Both Hitler and Stalin held definite views in

biology. Biologists who disagreed with Hitler's racial theories were not tolerated. Biologists who upheld the view that environment influences the genes were strongly supported in the USSR under Stalin, because this theory seemed to accord with Marxism-Leninism; biologists who espoused the contrary view (which was almost unanimously accepted outside the USSR) were often removed from their posts and exiled. Even linguists whose views conflicted with the pet theories of Stalin suffered. The social sciences are, of course, even more vulnerable to political and social persecution than the natural sciences. Mussolini and Hitler virtually wiped out the social sciences in Italy and Germany, as did Stalin in the USSR.

Assuming, then, that the Empiricists and the Trans-empiricists substantially agree on all these points, where do they differ? The genuine differences seem to be two. First, most Empirical Theorists hold that within all the limits just mentioned, it is possible to isolate and to test the empirical aspects of our beliefs about politics; whether the empirical propositions are true or false is entirely independent of our values. Going back to the five kinds of appraisal discussed earlier, the Empirical Theorist would argue that the first, second, and fourth primarily involve decisions about what *is* (in the sense of what is empirically true), whereas the third and the fifth primarily involve decisions about what *ought* to be. A "correct" decision on what is empirically true is not the same as a "correct" decision on what ought to be. To decide whether the hypothesis that acquired characteristics are transmitted through the genes is true or false is *logically* quite independent of any beliefs we may have about what ought to be; all the power Stalin could muster in behalf of the hypothesis did not make it *true*.

So too, the Empirical Theorist would argue, the truth or falsity of empirical propositions about politics does not logically depend on what we think ought to be but what in fact *is*. And no matter what that famous emperor thought or pretended to think, as he paraded before his subjects, he was not wearing any clothes! Other things being the same, are popular governments likely to be more unstable in countries where most of the population is illiterate than in countries where most people can read and write? Will increased elementary education raise or lower the chances of popular government in Indonesia? Does proportional representation produce multi-party systems? Does the two-party system require single-member districts? The answers to questions like these, Empirical Theorists argue, do not at all depend on what is right or good, what would be the best, or what one would prefer.

Many Trans-empirical Theorists would agree that fact and value are logically different, that knowledge of what *is* differs in important ways from knowledge of what ought to *be*. Some would argue that knowledge of what *is* also includes knowledge of man's "natural ends—ends toward which he is by nature inclined."[3] This, however, seems to reduce itself to a semantic point rather than a denial of the differences between statements of what *is* and statements of what *ought* to be. For if all people do in fact pursue their natural ends all the time, and are incapable of doing anything else, then human life is fully determined and it is useless to argue that they ought to do anything different from what they do do; but obviously the Trans-empiri-

[3] Leo Strauss, "Epilogue," in Herbert J. Storing (ed.), *Essays on the Scientific Study of Politics* (New York: Holt, Rinehart and Winston, 1962). This is the most extensive critique by Trans-empirical Theorists of the work of Empirical Theorists, and should be consulted for a fuller statement of their views.

cists do not believe this, since they hold that there are important moral choices in politics. But if one can say that people do not always pursue their "natural" ends, obviously it must be possible to distinguish what men do—the *is*—from what they *should* do—the *ought*. On this point common sense is heavily in accord with abstract reasoning.

However, most Trans-empiricists would argue that whatever the case might be in the natural sciences, facts and values are so intertwined in the study of politics that one cannot separate them except in the most trivial instances. Whatever one may pretend, they would say, one is making value judgments all the time. In the guise of neutrality and objectivity, the Empirical theorist smuggles in his own unacknowledged values. The very language of politics, the Trans-empiricists contend, is inescapably value-laden. And any comprehensive theory about politics, they would argue, must inevitably contain evaluations not merely of the empirical validity of the factual statements in the theory but also of the moral quality of the political events, processes, or systems described in the theory. Thus it is an illusion to think that a completely objective theory of politics can be created; if it were created, it would be so trivial as to be irrelevant.

Does this mean that students of politics cannot attain any neutrality and objectivity at all in their *empirical* analysis? Few if any Trans-empiricists would go so far. Is there, then, any real disagreement between the Empiricists and the Trans-empiricists on the importance of distinguishing between empirical analysis of what *is* from ethical analysis of what *ought* to be? It is, unfortunately, difficult to answer this question confidently. I believe, however, that a good deal of the argument is not really a dispute over the *logical* question whether the knowledge of what *is* in politics can be distinguished from knowledge of what *ought* to be, for with some exceptions both sides seem to agree that the *is* and the *ought* are logically distinguishable. Sometimes the dispute seems rather to turn on how much weight to give to all the qualifying factors mentioned above. In this case disagreement turns less on logical issues than on psychological ones; not whether fact and value are *logically* distinguishable but whether they are psychologically separable in political matters. Even more often, the dispute seems to turn not on whether fact and value *can* be distinguished but whether they *ought* to be separated in political analysis.

Facts and Values: Should Political Analysis Be Neutral?

In addition to doubting whether in practice a neutral, objective science of politics is possible, Trans-empiricists argue that a neutral science of politics is not even desirable.

We do not study politics, they would say, for esthetic reasons or for the joys of pure contemplation. We study politics in order to act rightly, to choose the best, to make decisions about how best to live with our fellow man—and therefore (as we have seen) we must appraise and evaluate. It is of no help to us to set our factual knowledge off to one side, neatly sealed up in an aseptic container, and values off to the other side, where they have no bearing on reality. Political appraisal is a constant interweaving of fact-finding and evaluation. The great political theorists of the past did not simply describe politics; they attempted to guide men in their search for a good life.

Political Evaluation

Trans-empiricists lodge four important charges against Empirical Theorists. Empirical Theorists, they say, have no criteria of relevance, since (as we have seen) these cannot be drawn simply from empirical knowledge. Hence, the Trans-empiricists contend, Empirical Political Theorists are prone to indulge in trivial investigations, irrelevant to human purposes. Second, they say, in striving for neutrality and objectivity, Empirical Theorists find it necessary to invent a new, complicated, and even ridiculous jargon. Third, in the attempt to eschew values, Empirical Theorists reject all grounds for evaluation and treat all values as equal. "By teaching the equality of all values," Leo Strauss writes, "by denying that there are things which are intrinsically high and others which are intrinsically low as well as by denying that there is an essential difference between men and brutes, it [Empirical Theory] contributes to the victory of the gutter."[4] Finally, while professing neutrality, Empirical Theorists are for the most part partisans of liberal democracy, and their "neutral" theories are frequently rationalizations for the values and practices of liberal democracy.

In reply, Empirical Theorists would agree that criteria of relevance and importance must be introduced if trivial inquiry is to be avoided, but they would contend that they have, in fact, used such criteria. They are concerned with many of the same questions that have animated political theorists from the beginning: the kinds of political systems, problems of stability, change, and revolution, the conditions of democracy and dictatorship, of war and peace, of equality and inequality, of freedom and slavery.

As to the second charge, Empirical Theorists are evidently not of one mind. Probably most Empirical Theorists would argue that the ordinary language of politics does pose serious problems, because many political terms in ordinary usage have a multiplicity of meanings—even among political scientists. Some Empirical Theorists, like Lasswell, have deliberately set out to develop as precise a vocabulary as possible. In doing so, they have drawn words from other social sciences and have re-defined older terms quite freely. To the uninitiated, Lasswell's writings seem, at first, strange and difficult. Other Empirical Theorists, however, strive to write without jargon. Moreover, the Trans-empiricists face the same problem and seem to be equally divided. Many Trans-empiricists use an unnatural vocabulary far removed from the ordinary language of politics; here, for example, is a sentence penned by one of the best known Trans-empiricists, Eric Voegelin: "The problems of an eidos in history, hence, arises only when Christian transcendental fulfillment becomes immanentized. Such an immanentist hypostasis of the eschaton, however, is a theoretical fallacy."[5]

Empirical Theorists reject the third charge as not only totally false but based on a baffling and persistent misreading of their writings and their assumptions.[6]

[4] Ibid., p. 326.
[5] The New Science of Politics: An Introductory Essay (Chicago: University of Chicago Press, 1952), p. 120. Voegelin's opening chapter represents one of the most severe indictments of Empirical Theory ever written by a Trans-empiricist.
[6] Max Weber is the particular bete noire of the Trans-empiricists. Thus Voegelin asserts that Weber "treated all values as equal" (ibid., p. 20); and Leo Strauss states that to Weber "all values are of the same rank," in Natural Right and History (Chicago: University of Chicago Press, 1953). For a full rebuttal of these assertions, see Brecht, op. cit., pp. 221–231 and 262–265.

Political Evaluation

The most plausible basis for the charge is that some Empirical Theorists have supported Logical Positivism; as we noted earlier some of the early Logical Positivists held that all value statements are "meaningless." It is doubtful, however, whether many Empirical Theorists in political science hold these extreme (and now somewhat old-fashioned views) of the early Logical Positivists. In any case there is no necessary connection between Empirical Theory and Logical Positivism. One does not need to espouse Logical Positivism in order to be an Empirical Theorist. Indeed, many different philosophical positions are consistent with Empirical Theory.

Certainly a theorist who attempts to develop neutral and objective empirical explanations of politics does not need to be indifferent to values. Most Empirical Theorists would argue that empirical knowledge is a necessary condition for wise moral choices. One may have very strong standards of right and wrong, but in order to apply them to political alternatives one must first know what is likely to result from choosing one alternative or the other. We do not apply morality in a vacuum; we apply our moral standards to the world of events. Hence it is important that so far as humanly possible we correctly understand what goes on in the world of events.

In reading Sophocles' great tragedy *Oedipus Rex* we do not arrive at a judgment of Oedipus simply by saying that parricide and incest are odious crimes. No more than Oedipus himself could we judge his actions unless we knew what he actually did. Did he slay his father? Is it true that the queen, his wife, is his mother? Did he consciously or unconsciously recognize who they were? These are (in principle) factual questions requiring factual answers first of all. Oedipus' relentless search for answers in the face of mounting evidence of how appalling the answers are going to be serves as a model for all time of a man who insists on knowing what is true in order to apply his standards of value, no matter what the costs may be. In the same way, the Empirical Theorist would argue, we cannot intelligently evaluate political systems unless we know how they operate. How can we say whether popular government is better than communism or military dictatorship for Americans, or Russians, or Turks unless we can predict with some confidence the main consequences for these peoples of the various alternatives? Factual knowledge is not a *substitute* for moral judgment, but it *is* a prerequisite.

As to the charge that they smuggle their own values into their theories and that these are usually liberal democratic values, the Empirical Theorists might respond something like this. Empirical Theorists probably do support democracy and open inquiry; even if there were no other reasons (and there are many), only popular governments seem to be capable of maintaining the freedom of inquiry necessary to Empirical Theory. Then, too, because empirical research is more easily carried on in polyarchies than in other systems, and also because the United States has been the modern center of empirical investigation of politics, Empirical Theorists have had more opportunity to do research on democratic political systems than on others. It is also true that certain aspects of popular systems such as the analysis of voting and public opinion are particularly amenable to study with rigorous modern methods.

To the extent that his values influence his selection of problems, provide him with important and relevant criteria, furnish him standards for evaluating alternative policies and systems, and permit him to take a position on controversial questions, the Empirical Theorist has no more need to

Political Evaluation

apologize for his values than the Trans-empirical Theorist. However, when his values bias his *empirical* findings, when his commitments to an *ought* distort his view of what *is,* then he would have to confess, *"Mea culpa!"* To the extent that this happens, he has failed to live up to his own standards. But this surely is no reason for abandoning these standards!

On the contrary (he might say): Every failure to provide an objective evaluation of the empirical aspects of politics is all the more reason for trying to develop a neutral and objective body of empirical theory. Would a doctor who failed to detect early cancer in one of his own children excuse himself on the ground that he loved his patient too much to make a correct diagnosis?

Ideas and Institutions

How are political ideas related to institutions? Answers to this question, too, are much disputed. Amid the welter of conflicting views it is possible to distinguish two fundamentally different types of explanation. The first I shall call a Rationalist explanation, the second a Materialist explanation.

A Rationalist explanation of the relation of political ideas to institutions gives primacy to the ways men think about politics. Institutions are man-made; unlike animals men can and do reason about their institutions; their institutions are shaped by their reasoning. Hence men's institutions can largely be explained as a product of the way men think about politics. Among civilized people, reasoning about politics is expressed in philosophical beliefs and attitudes that are most fully articulated by philosophers. But since men do not have equal power, it is the philosophical beliefs of the rulers that are particularly critical.

Thus a Rationalist explanation might be illustrated as follows:

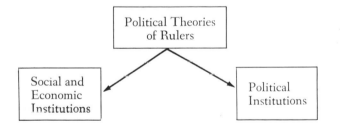

Rationalist explanations run into a number of serious objections. First, men do not reason in a vacuum. When they reason *about* their political, economic, and social institutions, they also reason *in* these institutions. Isn't their thinking shaped by their institutions? Second, if institutions are the product of reasoning, why is there so much conflict over institutions? The Rationalist might answer that conflict is caused by "bad reasoning"; in principle, he might argue (as Plato does in *Meno*) that when men reason together carefully they are bound to come to the same conclusion. But what causes "bad reasoning" about institutions, and hence conflict? Is "bad reasoning" simply an intellectual slip, like failing to understand the proof of a theorem in geometry? Or are not the causes of different ways of reasoning often produced by the way men live—that is, by their institutions? Third, is it pure accident that **107**

in conflicts over institutions, reason so often seems to bring each person to a conclusion that happens to jibe with his own material interests? Fourth, now that Freud and his successors have thoroughly documented what poets and dramatists have always known—that powerful unconscious forces often whip reason along like a feather in a windstorm—is it realistic to explain *any* aspect of human behavior as the work of pure reason?

Finally, doesn't the Rationalist explanation overestimate the normal human capacity for reasoning logically about abstract matters? To attribute political decisions to the political *theories* of rulers is often merely to dignify by the word "theory" a grab-bag of prejudices, inconsistencies, superficial impressions, and simple untutored impulses. Indeed, most people find it very difficult to think abstractly about politics at all. In one study of the 1956 presidential election in the United States, an attempt was made to classify citizens by the extent to which their answers concerning why they liked or disliked Eisenhower, Stevenson, the Republican party, and the Democratic party gave any evidence of "ideological" thinking. Even under the most generous interpretation, only about 1 out of 6 voters gave an answer that suggested his preferences were related in some way to ideological or philosophical abstractions of any sort. Almost half the voters explained their preferences simply on the basis that they or people like them would be better off with the one or the other. About a quarter simply responded in effect by saying that the times were good or bad.[7]

A Materialist explanation accepts these criticisms with a vengeance. It holds that political institutions and ideas can be explained by the play of material interests. The material interests of people are status, income and wealth. In general, people seek to gain more of these and to avoid losing what they have. In any given historical period, social and economic institutions may be taken as more or less fixed. The social and economic institutions allocate status, income, and wealth, which are also the principal resources of power. People who are awarded by the social and economic institutions of the time the highest status, income, and wealth (and hence the greatest power) use their power to protect these institutions. Hence they seek to develop political institutions that insure their own status, income, and wealth. They also search for ideologies that will make their rulership legitimate and hence more effective. But since social and economic institutions allocate status, income, and wealth unequally, people inconvenienced by the status quo may aspire to change the institutions in their own favor. They frequently develop counter-ideologies, revolutionary utopias that justify their own ultimate hopes of becoming rulers. Thus the way people think about politics is a rationalization or defense of the political, social, and economic institutions that they think will maximize their own material interests. Neither rulers nor ruled have much difficulty in finding intellectuals who will assist them in the grand task of designing a suitable ideology or utopia. Hence the history of political philosophy is a history of grandiose rationalizations for the material interests and power of rulers or for their opponents' aspirations for power, status, income, and wealth.

A Material explanation might be illustrated, then, like this:

[7] Angus Campbell, *et al.*, *The American Voter* (New York: Wiley, 1960), Table 10–1, p. 249.

Political Evaluation

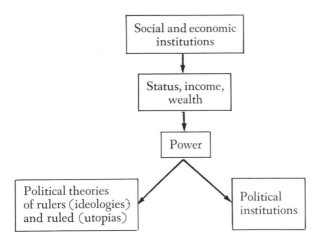

The great strength of the Materialist explanation is that it has its roots in ordinary experience and common sense. It is a hard-headed, unsentimental, no-nonsense appeal to realism. The ways in which men earn their bread, gain respect, and wield power obviously do influence their thinking about politics. Studies of voting and public opinion from industrialized countries all over the world show, for example, that "the lower-income groups vote mainly for parties of the left, while the higher-income groups vote mainly for parties of the right."[8] Surely this is not unrelated to the fact that the parties of the left promise reforms that will provide material benefits to the lower-income groups at the possible expense of upper-income groups!

Because of its common-sense appeal, the Materialist explanation has been advanced in one form or another, no doubt, ever since men began to think about politics. Plato attributed a Materialist explanation to Thrasymachus. Two millennia later, it was no more than obvious common sense to many of the men at the American Constitutional Convention. It acquired its most extreme and elaborate formulation at the hands of Marx and Engels. Today it is official gospel in many parts of the world, and unofficial gospel in others.

Nonetheless, there are some serious difficulties in the Materialist explanation. Of these, we shall consider what is probably the most important: the problem of "mis-identification."

It is an empirical fact that people who play similar roles in social and economic structures often conflict in their political ideas and goals. If urban workers are usually to the left of businessmen, in every country in which free elections are held a sizeable minority of the working classes supports non-working class parties. For example, it has been estimated that nearly half the votes for Conservative party candidates in the British general elections of 1945, 1950, and 1951 were cast by manual wage workers, and a fifth or more of the votes for Labor party candidates were drawn from the middle classes.[9] Moreover, the changing fortunes of the two parties in these elections did not result from marked shifts in the way different socio-economic classes voted but in *national* tides that swept through all the classes. When Labor

[8] Seymour M. Lipset, *Political Man* (New York: Doubleday, 1960), pp. 223–224.
[9] John Bonham, *The Middle Class Vote* (London: Faber and Faber, n.d.), Table 18, p. 168.

Political Evaluation

or Conservatism was on the upswing in the middle classes it was also on the upswing among the working classes.[10] It is an interesting fact, too, that people who are "objectively" in similar social and economic positions often do not see their positions in the same way. For example, among manual employees in Britain, nearly a third identify themselves as members of the middle classes; among white-collar office employees, about three-fourths identify themselves as middle class whereas a quarter identify themselves as working class.[11]

Materialists seek to explain this "mis-identification" on the ground that some people fail to identify their social and economic position "correctly." They could point out that in Britain and the United States blue-collar workers who identify themselves as "working class" are likely to vote differently from those who identify themselves as "middle class."[12] But why do people in similar *objective* socio-economic positions identify themselves subjectively in different ways? The Materialist would have to say: because some of them do not *reason* correctly about their experiences and their society.

Thus simply in order to account for the plain facts of experience—among others the fact of "mis-identification"—the Materialist must re-admit reasoning into the process by which individuals make their decisions. But if individuals can reason about their decisions, obviously they can reason differently about what are their *true* interests, their proper goals, the nature of the good life. Hence, although Materialism appears to reject the Rationalist explanation entirely, it re-admits some elements of Rationalism by the back door. What happens if material goals conflict? Is there some kind of pre-ordained hierarchy of material goals? If so, how has this hierarchy been established? If not, cannot people disagree whether they should prefer, say, wealth to power? Finally, if individuals can reason about their decisions, why must they necessarily conclude that their material interests—status, wealth, income, power—are their only values or even their most important values?

Thus if the Rationalist explanation of the relation between ideas and institutions seems inadequate because it does not satisfactorily account for the influence of institutions on ideas, the Materialist explanation seems inadequate because it does not account for the influence of ideas on institutions. Although these two explanations have been presented here in somewhat simplified form (and although there are other explanations than these two) it is fair to say that the relations between political ideas and institutions are still imperfectly understood and a matter of sharp controversy.

[10] *Ibid.*, p. 162.

[11] *Ibid.*, p. 60. For similar results in the United States, see Richard Centers, *The Psychology of Social Classes* (Princeton: Princeton University Press, 1949).

[12] Bonham, *op. cit.*, p. 180, and Campbell, *et al., op. cit.*, Table 13–9, p. 371.

Political Evaluation

To Explore Further

The study of politics holds much of the shape given to it by Aristotle, whose epochal works on politics and ethics are models of breadth and depth. *The Politics of Aristotle* is, fortunately, available in a highly readable contemporary translation with introduction, notes, and appendices by Ernest Barker (New York and London, Oxford University Press, 1948).

Aristotle greatly profited from his gifted teacher, Plato, whose *Republic* has excited endless generations of students by its beauty, grace, imagination, and intellectual power. *The Republic* is available in a number of translations that sometimes differ from one another in disconcerting ways. The most recent is *The Republic of Plato,* translated with introduction and notes by F. M. Cornford (New York and London: Oxford University Press, 1945). In these two works Plato and Aristotle asked most of the important, interesting, and persistent questions about politics that have been of concern to students of politics ever since.

Comprehensive modern works on political analysis are rare. In the text, the modern writers most frequently cited are Max Weber and Harold D. Lasswell. Neither, alas, is easy reading for the beginner. A good deal of Weber's work has been translated into English. Of particular relevance to political analysis is *The Theory of Social and Economic Organization,* translated by A. M. Henderson and Talcott Parsons, and edited with an introduction by Parsons (New York: Oxford University Press, 1947), Part III, "The Types of Authority and Imperative Coordination." See also *From Max Weber: Essays in Sociology,* translated, edited, and with an introduction by H. H. Gerth and C. Wright Mills (New York: Oxford University Press, 1946). The most readable of Lasswell's general works is his *Politics: Who Gets What, When, How* (New York: McGraw-Hill, 1936).

Modern efforts to develop comprehensive theories of politics, in addition to those discussed in the next section, include: C. E. Merriam, *Systematic Politics* (Chicago: University of Chicago Press, 1945); Ernest Barker, *Reflections on Government* (New York: Oxford University Press, 1942); and G. E. G. Catlin, *The Science and Method of Politics* (New York: Knopf, 1927).

There are a number of descriptive, critical, or analytical summaries of political science as a field of inquiry. *Contemporary Political Science* (Paris, Unesco, 1950) tries to summarize the state of political studies throughout the world. Dwight Waldo provides a special analysis for the United States in *Political Science in the United States of America, A Trend Report* (Paris, Unesco, 1956). A searching and thoughtful criticism is contained in David Easton, *The Political System, An Inquiry into the State of Political Science* (New York: Knopf, 1953). See also Charles Hyneman, *The Study of Politics* (Urbana: University of Illinois Press, 1959); Vernon Van Dyke, *Political Science: A Philosophical Analysis* (Stanford: Stanford University Press, 1960); and *Research Frontiers in Politics and Government* (Washington, D.C.: The Brookings Institution, 1955).

The central sections of Aristotle's *Politics* classify political systems into different types and attempt to explain the conditions of stability and change. In the Barker edition, cited above, these sections are Book III, "The Theory of Citizenship and Constitutions"; Book IV, "Actual Constitutions and Their Varieties"; Book V, "Causes of Revolution and Constitutional Change"; and Book VI, "Methods of Constructing Democracies and Oligarchies with a View to Stability."

In recent American political science, what Aristotle undertook in these four books of *The Politics* generally goes under the name of Comparative Government. Although there are innumerable texts bearing the label Comparative Government, most of them consist of descriptions of different national systems without much comparison or theory. Among the principal exceptions have been Carl J. Friedrich, *Constitutional Government and Democracy* (Boston: Ginn, 1941); R. M. MacIver, *The Web of Government* (New York: Macmillan, 1947); and F. G. Wilson, *The Elements of Modern Politics* (New York: McGraw-Hill, 1936). The volume in this series by Dankwart Rustow, tentatively titled *Comparative Government* (Englewood Cliffs, N.J.: Prentice-Hall, forthcoming) will also emphasize similarities and differences among political systems.

The analysis of political systems is a rapidly growing field, particularly in the United States, whose emergence as a world power has suddenly confronted scholars and policy-makers with the urgent need to find answers to the kinds of questions Aristotle was also seeking to answer. A significant, brief, and highly readable work in the new spirit is Roy C. Macridis, *The Study of Comparative Government* (Garden City, N.Y.: Doubleday, 1955). Far and away the most influential recent work is the volume edited by Gabriel A. Almond and James S. Coleman, *The Politics of the Developing Areas* (Princeton: Princeton University Press, 1960); see particularly the opening chapter by Almond and the concluding chapter by Coleman. For a short and frequently cited recent essay, see David Easton "An Approach to the Analysis of Political Systems," *World Politics*, Vol. 9 (1956–1957), pp. 383–400.

Although notions of influence, power, and authority have been important elements in political analysis since Plato and Aristotle, until recently few political analysts made serious attempts to clarify these concepts. The chief exception was the English philosopher Thomas Hobbes (1588–1679), who examined the concept of power with considerable precision in his great work, *Leviathan or the Matter, Forme and Power of a Commonwealth, Ecclesiasticall and Civil* which is available with an introduction by Michael Oakeshott (New York: Macmillan, 1947). The most influential modern writer is Lasswell; cf. his highly abstract work with Abraham Kaplan, *Power and Society* (New Haven: Yale University Press, 1950). Felix E. Oppenheim, *Dimensions of Freedom* (New York: St. Martin's Press, 1961) sets out clearly, though, like Lasswell abstractly, a number of concepts concerning control, power, and freedom. A succinct discussion of a number of problems in observing and measuring power is Herbert Simon's "Notes on the Observation and Measurement of Political Power," *Journal of Politics,* Vol. 15, No. 4 (November, 1953), pp. 500–516. Somewhat more difficult is James G. March "An Introduction to the Theory and Measurement of Influence," *American Political Science Review,* Vol. 49, No. 2 (June, 1955), pp. 431–451. Several attempts have been made to give mathematical form to measurements of power, including Robert A. Dahl, "The Concept of Power,"

Behavioral Science, Vol. 2, No. 3 (July, 1957), pp. 201–215; and John C. Harsanvi, "Measurement of Social Power, Opportunity Costs, and the Theory of Two-Person Bargaining Games," *Behavioral Science,* Vol. 7, No. 1 (January, 1962), pp. 67–80. However, the beginning student is well-advised to pass these by unless he has a consuming interest in mathematics.

It is worth mentioning Bertrand Russell's rather widely known book *Power* (New York: Norton, 1938) by way of warning that it is highly disappointing to anyone looking for conceptual clarity, though it contains some interesting ideas about various forms of rule.

Some of the most important recent work on influence and power consists of empirical studies using a variety of different methods and theories, particularly of local communities. Floyd Hunter's *Community Power Structure* (Chapel Hill: University of North Carolina Press, 1953) has been highly influential and much criticized. Another volume of great influence is the late C. Wright Mills' *The Power Elite* (New York: Oxford University Press, 1957). A criticism of Hunter and Mills and suggestions for a different approach will be found in Robert A. Dahl, "A Critique of the Ruling Elite Model," *American Political Science Review,* Vol. 52, No. 2 (June, 1958), pp. 463–469; and *Who Governs?* (New Haven: Yale University Press, 1961).

For criticism of some of the recent work on power, see Barrington Moore, Jr., *Political Power and Social Theory* (Cambridge, Mass.: Harvard University Press, 1958).

Perhaps the most influential book ever written on the characteristics of men in politics is *The Prince,* by the great Renaissance Italian Nicolo Machiavelli (1469–1527). Despite its enduring popularity, fascination, and authority it is extremely one-sided and unsystematic. *The Prince* is available in many forms; a single volume entitled *The Prince and The Discourses,* with an introduction by Max Lerner (New York: The Modern Library, 1940) has the advantage of including Machiavelli's most substantial though much less well-known work, *Discourses on the First Ten Books of Titus Livius.* More systematic in its treatment of political man than *The Prince,* though about equally one-sided, is Hobbes' first section of *The Leviathan* entitled "Of Man." Hobbes' psychological assumptions bear a remarkable resemblance to the modern school of psychology often called Behaviorism.

Probably the most influential contemporary writer on political man is Lasswell, who brings to his studies the training and theories of a psychoanalyst. Lasswell's early work, *Psychopathology and Politics* (Chicago: University of Chicago Press, 1930), is a pioneering work that remains rewarding reading. The most extensive statement of his more recent views is contained in *Power and Personality* (New York: Norton, 1948). Where Lasswell relied on clinical evidence covering a few individuals, the development of scientific sample surveys of public opinion has made it possible to acquire extensive if often more superficial knowledge of the political views and activities of different segments of the general population. The most comprehensive summary and analysis of survey results is Robert Lane, *Political Life* (Glencoe, Ill.: The Free Press, 1959). Some of the essays of S. M. Lipset in his collection entitled *Political Man* (New York: Doubleday, 1960) also use survey data to explore the characteristics of *homo politicus.* There has been a series of studies of electoral participation and attitudes of voters in elections both here and abroad; the most recent and most comprehensive is A. Campbell, *et al., The American Voter* (New York: Wiley, 1960).

To Explore Further

Some writers have recently tried to probe political man much more deeply than survey methods permit, by analyzing lengthy interviews with a small number of individuals—e.g., M. Brewster Smith, Jerome S. Bruner and Robert W. White, *Opinions and Personality* (New York: Wiley, 1956); and Robert E. Lane, *Political Ideology: Why the American Common Man Believes What He Does* (Glencoe, Ill.: The Free Press, 1962).

In approaching the concepts of conflict and stability, probably the best starting point is Book V of Aristotle's *Politics,* cited above: "Causes of Revolutions and Constitutional Change."

In *The Functions of Social Conflict* (London: Routledge and Kegan Paul, 1956) Lewis Coser seeks to bring up to date the contributions to the study of conflict of the German sociologist Georg Simmel; Coser emphasizes the mechanisms of conflict and adjustment more than the conditions and causes of conflict. R. Dahrendorf, *Class and Class Conflict in Industrial Societies* (Stanford: Stanford University Press, 1959) examines the relevance of the Marxian analysis of class structures in what he calls "post-capitalist" societies. In *Organizations* (New York: Wiley, 1958) J. March and H. Simon focus in several chapters on problems of conflict and adjustment in organizations; cf. especially Chapter 5, "Conflict in Organizations."

James Coleman, *Community Conflict* (Glencoe, Ill.: The Free Press, 1957), brings together a large number of studies of conflicts in American communities, analyzes them with considerable insight, and suggests a theory to explain the rise and course of conflicts in communities.

The prerequisites for stability of popular governments are examined in Almond and Coleman, *The Politics of the Developing Areas,* and in Lipset's *Political Man,* particularly Part I, "The Conditions of the Democratic Order." By intensively studying a trade union with a well-developed two-party system, Lipset, Coleman, and M. A. Trow develop highly relevant data and theory about the conditions of stable democracy in *Union Democracy, The Internal Politics of the International Typographers Union* (Glencoe, Ill.: The Free Press, 1956).

The ancient question explored by Plato, of the relationship between different kinds of political systems and different kinds of character or personality, occupies an important place in modern political analysis. *The Authoritarian Personality* by T. W. Adorno, Else Frenkel-Brunswik, Daniel J. Levinson, and R. Nevitt Sanford (New York: Harper, 1950) is psychoanalytic in its approach and has stimulated a vast amount of new research and analysis, some of it critical. See, for example, R. Christie and Marie Jahoda (eds.), *Studies in the Scope and Method of "The Authoritarian Personality"* (Glencoe, Ill.: The Free Press, 1954). The exact relation between personality factors and specific political acts is a matter of considerable dispute. Campbell, *et al.,* in *The American Voter,* express doubt that personality is closely related to voting choices; see Chapter 18, "Personality Factors in Voting Behavior." On more comprehensive ideological orientations toward democracy, communism, conservatism, and reformism, the connections seem to be clearer. See, for example, Herbert McCloskey, "Conservatism and Personality," *American Political Science Review,* Vol. 52, No. 1 (March, 1958), pp. 27–45; Gabriel A. Almond, *The Appeals of Communism* (Princeton: Princeton University Press, 1954); and Lipset, "Working Class Authoritarianism," in *Political Man.*

Political evaluation and decision are, as Chapter 8 of this text indicates, matters of considerable controversy. Most of the writing on this question is

To Explore Further

either highly technical or highly polemical. Nonetheless, one can gain a fair picture of the issues and proposed answers by consulting several of the following. Arnold Brecht's *Political Theory, The Foundations of Twentieth Century Political Thought* (Princeton: Princeton University Press, 1959) is an extensive statement of the issues, the history of the conflict, the different views, and his own position, which he calls Scientific Value Relativism. T. D. Weldon, *The Vocabulary of Politics* (Harmondsworth, England: Penguin Books, 1953) takes a position somewhat like that of Brecht.

The most thoroughgoing criticism of the Empiricist position is contained in Herbert J. Storing (ed.), *Essays on the Scientific Study of Politics* (New York: Holt, Rinehart and Winston, 1961), which contains four essays critically examining the voting studies and the theories of Herbert Simon, Arthur F. Bentley and Harold Lasswell, together with a final essay by Leo Strauss. Perhaps the most important statement by a leading Trans-empiricist is Leo Strauss' *Natural Right and History* (Chicago: University of Chicago Press, 1953). See also Erich Voegelin's highly polemical essay, *The New Science of Politics* (Chicago: University of Chicago Press, 1952).

Some aspects of the debate will be found in the exchange between F. E. Oppenheim "The Natural Law Thesis," H. Jaffa, "Comment on Oppenheim," and Oppenheim's "Non-Cognitivist Rebuttal," all in the *American Political Science Review*, Vol. 51, No. 1 (March, 1957), pp. 41–68.

In order to thread his way through this difficult and sometimes tedious debate, the beginner may find it helpful to consult a standard text on ethics— for example, W. Sellers and J. Hospers (eds.), *Readings in Ethical Theory* (New York: Appleton-Century-Crofts, 1952), or L. J. Binkley, *Contemporary Ethical Theories* (New York: Citadel Press, 1961). Some understanding of the nature of modern science as interpreted by contemporary philosophers of science is also useful. Probably the best elementary text is Morris R. Cohen and Ernest Nagel, *An Introduction to Logic and Scientific Method* (New York: Harcourt, Brace, 1934). A delightful statement of what science is all about by a writer who happens to be both a physicist and a successful playwright is Jacob Bronowski, *The Common Sense of Science* (Cambridge, Mass.: Harvard University Press, 1953). Difficult but rewarding are Herbert Feigl and May Brodbeck (eds.), *Readings in the Philosophy of Science* (New York: Appleton-Century-Crofts, 1953); Karl Popper, *The Logic of Scientific Discovery* (New York: Basic Books, 1959); R. B. Braithwaite, *Scientific Explanation* (Cambridge, England: Cambridge University Press, 1953); and Ernest Nagel, *The Structure of Science* (New York: Harcourt, Brace and World, 1961), especially Chapters 13, "Methodological Problems of the Social Sciences"; 14, "Explanation and Understanding in the Social Sciences"; and 15, "Problems in the Logic of Historical Inquiry."

To Explore Further

Index

Index

Index